© 2018 Nas E. Boutammina
Illustration : Nas E. Boutammina
Traduction : Elie Skenaz

Edition : BoD - Books on Demand
12/14 rond-point des Champs Elysées 75008 Paris
Imprimé par BoD - Books on Demand, Norderstedt
ISBN : 9782322104086
Dépôt légal : février 2018

Notes of the translator

Elie Skenaz is a translator, writer and a foreign language trainer with a background of more than 20 years teaching French. She has translated technical and scientific books from English to French and French to English and is currently working on a biography translation of Historical Figures.

She holds a Master degree in French literature from the University of Houston, Texas and a Master degree in Molecular Biology from the University of Paris XI, Orsay. She speaks fluently English, French and Arabic.

After having read for the first time Nas. Boutammina, I was quite skeptical about this historic vision that shake our knowledge. Being myself from a scientific background and literature, I wanted to check some historical data that were presented. Gradually my research and reading aimed me not only to see in his work valid arguments but to date no argument against it has ever emerged.

Nevertheless, as a translator, my primary role is to report the primary source into French to English-speaking audience and therefore, my personal opinion on the subject should in any way interfere. These are the words of the author who must reach the audience and not the translator's.

This work was a challenge because of wanting to bring one who has clearly denounced translators and plagiarists in history was in itself a laborious and painstaking work in linguistic research. We must add that Mr. Boutammina has a personal style that uses a large number of neologisms as wanting to restore truth, the words themselves have lost their primary meaning and therefore what it must redefine [and you can record the lengthy footnotes] or create terms that are more conducive to the accuracy of his thought.

An industrious and ingenious work that I have had the honor to do in translating it to present it to an English audience who will certainly appreciate this new vision of the history of science to be able to restore historical truth. This work is a first step towards questioning and reflecting on our history and will for years to come to be included in all educational and academic works to restore historical truth.

Elie Skenaz

Biography of the writer

Nas Boutammina is a French author with doctoral training in Biological and Medical Sciences.

His scientific research during his graduate study has naturally led to interest in the History of Science, namely that of Medicine, discussed widely on college campuses. This intellectual development and curiosity inevitably led Dr. Boutammina to study a variety of other disciplines, including the Humanities [History, Anthropology...] Theology, and the Experimental Sciences.

Dr. Boutammina erects a new discipline altogether: Anthropology of Islam, which is an entirely novel approach to Prehistory, Archaeology, Anthropology and Paleontology.

Gifted with a critical spirit and excellent insight, the author advances his investigations so as to apprehend the fields of Knowledge. His work, on the one hand, casts light on the shadier aspects of human knowledge, bringing to light different perspectives from those commonly admitted; on the other, Dr. Boutammina enriches the whole of human Knowledge with the innovation of new theories, categories, and concepts.

Table of Contents

Notes of the translator

Biography of the writer

Table of Contents

Works by Nas, Boutammina [in French]

Introduction

I - What is Retabulism ?
  A - Generalities 31
    1 - Retabulism - Retabulist - Definition 31
      a - Retabulism [Re-establishment] 31
      b - Retabulist 31
      c - Retabulism and the retabulist proposal 33
      d - Retabulist Values 34
      e - The subject of Retabulism 35
        - The relationship between Retabulism and knowledge 36
        - Re-establishing the predefined 37
      f - Meaning and Retabulism 40
        - The test of the significance of Retabulism 41
        - Pragmatist Retabulism 45
      g - Retabulism and its perception 47
        - Retabulism and Reality 47
        - Truth, Retabulism's quests 48

II - Historical and Historiographical Retabulism: a scholarly textual criticism
  A - Definition of Terms 51
    1 - History 51
      a - Historian 51
      b - Historiography 51

2 - The Value of Historiography 51
3 - Historiographical Retabulism 52
4 - Classical Islamic Civilization or CIC [eighth-fourteenth century] 52
   a - Definition..52
   b - Error-proofing Retabulism 56
5 - Historical Retabulism in popular culture 56
6 - Axiomatic historical Retabulism 56
7 - Historical Laws of historical Retabulism 58
8 - Retabulism and the likelihood of facts.......................61
9 - Epistemological Design of Retabulism......................63
   a - Retabulism: the intellectualist activity...................64
   b - Sociology of Retabulism..66
      - Retabulism and the dissemination of knowledge 67

III - Theological Retabulism
   A - The Idea of Formal Theological Retabulist Knowledge 72
      1 - Retabulism and Theological Liberation 73
         a - The Tradition : A Rebellion against Reason 75
      2 - The Axiom of Theological Retabulism 78
      3 - The Logical-Theological Notion of Retabulism........80
      4 - Retabulism and Theological Knowledge...................83
      5 - Analytical Retabulism 85
      6 - The Epistemo-Retabulist Aspect................................87
         a - The proposal and the fact..87
         b - Evidentiary Devices...89
         c - Proof and Justification 90
      7 - Supratheology : Schism and Heresy 94
         a - The Traditionalist Conviction 94

IV - Retabulism of a Universal Order : Being in the service of Humanity
   A - The Idealo-Realism of Retabulism 97
      1 - Retabulism and Functional Construction of Consciousness 100
         a - Retabulism and Historicism................................ 102
            - Resistance to change... 103

b - Retabulism and Truth.. 104
c - Retabulism of He who Reflects........................... 108
2 - Retabulism and the Future of Human Society...... 110
a - The Outlook of Retabulism................................ 114
3 - Themes or topics that may be addressed by Retabulism
.... 117
a - Some Prospective Retabulist Tracks................... 118
- Prehistory 118
- Antiquity 118
- Middle Ages and Renaissance............................. 118
- Enlightenment 119
- Modern Era 119

Annex

Conclusion

Alphabetical index

Works by Nas, Boutammina [in French]

- NAS E. BOUTAMMINA, « Y-a-t-il eu un temple de Salomon à Jérusalem ? », Edit. BoD, Paris [France], aout 2011.
- NAS E. BOUTAMMINA, « Les ennemis de l'Islam - Le règne des Antésulmans - Avènement de l'Ignorance, de l'Obscurantisme et de l'Immobilisme », Edit. BoD, Paris [France], avril 2010, 2ᵉ édition février 2012.
- NAS E. BOUTAMMINA, « Le secret des cellules immunitaires - Théorie bouleversant l'Immunologie [The secrecy of immune cells - Theory upsetting Immunologie] », Edit. BoD, Paris [France], mars 2012.
- NAS E. BOUTAMMINA, « Le Livre bleu - I - Du discours social », Edit. BoD, Paris [France], juillet 2014.
- NAS E. BOUTAMMINA, « Le Rétablisme », Edit. BoD, Paris [France], septembre 2013, 2ᵉ édition mars 2015.
- NAS E. BOUTAMMINA, « Comprendre la Renaissance - Falsification et fabrication de l'Histoire de l'Occident », Edit. BoD, Paris [France], août 2013, 2ᵉ édition avril 2015.
- NAS E. BOUTAMMINA, « Connaissez-vous l'Islam ? », Edit. BoD, Paris [France], mars 2010, 2ᵉ édition avril 2015.
- NAS E. BOUTAMMINA, « Le Malāk, entité de l'Invisible », Edit. BoD, Paris [France], mai 2015.
- NAS E. BOUTAMMINA, « Jésus fils de Marie ou Hiyça ibn Māryām ? », Edit. BoD, Paris [France], janvier 2010, 2ᵉ édition juin 2015.
- NAS E. BOUTAMMINA, « Index Historum Prohibitorum », Edit. BoD, Paris [France], juin 2015.
- NAS E. BOUTAMMINA, « Moïse ou Moūwça ? », Edit. BoD, Paris [France], janvier 2010, 2ᵉ édition juin 2015.
- NAS E. BOUTAMMINA, « Mahomet ou Moūhammad ? », Edit. BoD, Paris [France], mars 2010, 2ᵉ édition juin 2015.
- NAS E. BOUTAMMINA, « Abraham ou Ibrāhiym ? », Edit. BoD, Paris [France], février 2010, 2ᵉ édition juin 2015.
- NAS E. BOUTAMMINA, « Musulmophobie - Origines ontologique et psychologique », Edit. BoD, Paris [France], décembre 2009, 2ᵉ édition juillet 2015.

- Nas E. Boutammina, « Les Jinn bâtisseurs de pyramides… ? », Edit. BoD, Paris [France], juin 2009, 2ᵉ édition septembre 2015.
- Nas E. Boutammina, « La Mort - Approche anthropologique et eschatologique », Edit. BoD, Paris [France], novembre 2015.
- Nas E. Boutammina, « Les contes des mille et un mythes - Volume I », [Edit. Originale 1 vol. août 1999]. Edit. BoD, Paris [France], juillet 2011, 2ᵉ édition février 2017.
- Nas E. Boutammina, « Les contes des mille et un mythes - Volume II », [Edit. Originale 1 vol. août 1999]. Edit. BoD, Paris [France], novembre 2011, 2ᵉ édition février 2017.
- Nas E. Boutammina, « Le Jinn, créature de l'Invisible », Edit. BoD, Paris [France], décembre 2010, 2ᵉ édition février 2017.
- Nas E. Boutammina, « Sociologie du Français musulman - Perspectives d'avenir ? », Edit. BoD, Paris [France], mai 2011, 2ᵉ édition février 2017.
- Nas E. Boutammina, « Judéo-christianisme - Le mythe des mythes ? », Edit. BoD, Paris [France], juin 2011, 2ᵉ édition mars 2017.
- Nas E. Boutammina, « De l'abomination de la Politique, des politiciens et des partis », Edit. BoD, Paris [France], mars 2018.
- Nas E. Boutammina, « Une société sans politicien, sans parti politique - Concours National aux Fonctions de l'Appareil Etatique [CNFAE] », Edit. BoD, Paris [France], mars 2018.

Collection Néo-anthropologie [Anthropologie de l'Islam]

- Nas E. Boutammina, « Apparition de l'Homme - Modélisation islamique - Volume I », Edit. BoD, Paris [France], août 2010, 2ᵉ édition juillet 2015.
- Nas E. Boutammina, « L'Homme, qui est-il et d'où vient-il ? - Volume II », Edit. BoD, Paris [France], octobre 2010, 2ᵉ édition juillet 2015.
- Nas E. Boutammina, « Classification islamique de la Préhistoire - Volume III », Edit. BoD, Paris [France], novembre 2010, 2ᵉ édition juillet 2015.
- Nas E. Boutammina, « Expansion de l'Homme sur la Terre depuis son origine par mouvement ondulatoire - Volume IV », Edit. BoD, Paris [France], novembre 2010, 2ᵉ édition juillet 2015.

- Nas E. Boutammina, « Le Kaabaéen prototype des systèmes d'écriture » - Volume V », Edit. BoD, Paris [France], avril 2016, 2ᵉ édition mai 2016.
- Nas E. Boutammina, « Industries, vestiges archéologiques et préhistoriques - Action aléatoire de la nature & Action intentionnelle de l'Homme » - Volume VI », Edit. BoD, Paris [France], juillet 2016.

Collection Œuvres universelles de l'Islam

- Nas E. Boutammina, « Les Fondateurs de la Chimie », Edit. BoD, Paris [France], octobre 2013.
- Nas E. Boutammina Nas E. Boutammina, « Les Fondateurs de la Pharmacologie », Edit. BoD, Paris [France], novembre 2014.
- Nas E. Boutammina, « Les Fondateurs de la Médecine », Edit. BoD, Paris [France], septembre 2011, 2ᵉ édition mars 2017.
- Nas E. Boutammina, « Les Fondateurs de la Botanique », Edit. BoD, Paris [France], mai 2017.

Nas. E. Boutammina

The Retabulism

Translation into English from French

By Elie Skenaz

Introduction

The Retabulism appears in a scientific context strongly permeated by the development of the various disciplines of the Human Sciences, those of the experimental sciences, through the techniques of formal treatment of information. These are structured around concepts-pivots and animated by ideas-forces or fundamental assumptions attractions to the profound nature of the history and historiography (History of Science, theology, Tradition, etc.] erected in dogmas, which represents their object of study. The Retabulism is announced by its manner of disclosing their inaccuracy, their lies, their making.

The Retabulism asked in the very conception of the history and historiography the question of their true purpose, of their delimitation, of their specificity and their foundations. Therefore, it is impossible today, given the current state of misinformation and *Pithed ruminant carcasses* of earth, to keep, to describe this area, to a "history" type definition [Official History orthodox] and attempt to reach an intellectual design perfectly sensible, rational, and in sum authentic.

Finally, the problematic status of the historical accuracy of the events or facts asked questions of epistemological approaches that the Retabulism must absolutely elucidate by works which will heavily rely on the experimental survey and generally litigants as a scientific evaluation.

If the Retabulist plunged to the sources of the main scientific disciplines of modern times, it is to demonstrate by a rigorous argument the assertions that it supports.

The logic retabulist made during this time of manipulation of information, of essential conceptual tools and techniques in order to form a framework in which can be reflected in both the formalism and the History brought to a high degree of generality and of *operativity*.

The Retabulism gathers most of the ingredients necessary for the implementation of the great project of explanation of historical events past and present which are derived from the cultural heritages of the contemporary societies: it is nothing less than to replace the "*pendulum to the hour*". It is indeed here that the Retabulism draws a good part of his initial inspiration: enrich its directory of ideas which question the *official history*, this story manufactured and institutionalized for centuries and which remains the cultural foundation of contemporary societies.

I - What is Retabulism?

A - Generalities

1 - Retabulism - Retabulist - Definition

a -Retabulism [Re-establishment]

The expression "*to re-establish*" comes from the word restore which is defined as follows*: to return to the initial state; to a prior condition; to a normal state; to the authentic state; or to cause to exist again. The definition includes returning something [a notion, concept, idea, thought, science, knowledge, art, etc.] to that of which that something has been deprived.*

b -Retabulist

Refers to an individual who is in favor of Retabulism, or campaigns for Retabulism currents of thought. Adhering to Retabulism ideology, advocating Retabulism; member [s] of Retabulism. In general, it is a struggle to uphold an idea, a theory, or doctrine of Retabulism. By extension, it means a word that qualifies a noun [e.g., a Retabulism position, a Retabulism speech, Retabulism thought, etc.].

2 - Definition of Retabulism

A literary and artistic, school of thought or intellectual movement, mainly characterized by the refusal of any intellectual, aesthetic or moral consideration of *orthodox*

History, the weight given to the historical quest for scientific textual criticism, The monolithic control of history by Europe, or *Historeupean* or *Historeupéocentrism*. This term describes a History and Historiography essentially written and rewritten by Europe and focused, accordingly, on its *Greco-Roman Heritage*.

The goal of Retabulism is to discover a higher reality by seeking factual authenticity, using various methods: a multidisciplinary scientific consensus, the creation of study circles, a systematic and general exploration of texts, various means of communication, and comparing findings with other schools of thought that share the same hopes and the same quest.

Retabulism advocates free-thinking: independence of the individual mind with respect to historical and religious dogmas. By extension, Retabulism is an intellectual doctrine of historical truth; a warranty against any kind of incoherent dogmatism - against the arbitrary authority of economic monopolies or oligopolies adhering to a single ideology [such as Orthodox history/government]. Retabulism is thus also a tendency to progress, on a spiritual quest or to a higher truth!

Retabulism is a return to the authentic state of that which has been altered, or disingenuously re-possessed by *Orthodox History*. To better understand Retabulism, a field of study such as History of *Classical Islamic Civilization* helps illustrate the comments. In other words, CIC will serve as a background or thread to a more general explanation of Retabulism. Therefore, Retabulism aims to reconstruct all or part of this history of which original features have been transformed, diminished or removed as it passed through Ecclesiastical, secular [monarchs, bourgeoisie, etc.]or Zionist circuits. Retabulism aims to reclaim what gives Islam its originality; namely, its *Universalism*[i.e. "*Being in the service of humanity*"] and the quest for knowledge, Knowledge [Science] it inspires.

Retabulism restores honor to the too long forgotten illustrious figures of *Classical Islamic Civilization*, reclaiming a cultural heritage that, for many centuries, was cloistered in the Ignorance, Obscurantism and Immobilism of those who availed themselves of Islam.

Finally, Retabulism gives back to humanity what was stripped from it, a piece of its history; of *universal Culture*. Returning to this civilizational pattern to draw observations, and lessons from a period of planetary disorder and global bankruptcy.

Retabulism encourages and supports any action, transaction, proposal or idea - whatever its origin or allegiance - that strives to restore accuracy, authenticity, or integrity to any act; produced or imagined, broadcast and/or institutionalized!

c - Retabulism and the retabulist proposal

The term "*retabulist*" has at least several meanings. In the broadest sense, a proposal is called *retabulist* if it employs observation, analysis and argument to question any seemingly illogical idea or preconceived concept, extirpated [by virtue of the meaning it conveys] from reality - and thus of truth - and imposed as dogma. Thus, a retabulist proposal is commendable as guided by truth and universal [absolute] values.

All Retabulist truth requires reason and common sense. We say a judgment is Retabulist when it is conceptually implicit; knowledge entails discernment of imposture, false invention, or deceit.

An idea, concept or Retabulist thought quests for truth, for the logical, or that which is reducible to well-founded logic through cognition or reflection [thinking that is not a priori]. To establish the relevance of a Retabulist proposal, one simply refers to the meanings and general laws of logic and reason. Note that, due to its use of science and reflection, one condition of Retabulist action is that it demonstrates properties of universality. Any Retabulist proposal seeking truth is universal, in the sense that it does not depend on those who've obscured or retracted the truth.

d - Retabulist Values

Reflecting on Retabulism is neither a speculative nor abstract activity. It is circumscribed by the adequacy of the scientific mind and often with the idea of God, as a safeguard between the human mind and the universe that surrounds it. Retabulism is defined by the agreement of minds together for a common goal: the truth that is reality. *"Being in the service of humanity"* is its constant concern. Every human is or should be a Retabulist due to the individual's intrinsic relationship with all humanity. We should also mention that the Retabulist criterion is success in the actions it lays claim to. Being attached to the past,

Retabulism requires true judgments, proposals, etc. in determining its [ethical, aesthetic, etc.] values.

e - The subject of Retabulism

Retabulism is the opposite of falsehood, dissimulation, lying. The meaning of the word '*Retabulism*' must here be understood in its full sense. But the word needs to be clarified. The logician must often make sense of a reflexive dynamic: "*rigorous reasoning rigorously.*" We only say that it seems unacceptable to attribute to Retabulism any laxity [intellectual laziness, complacency, carelessness] in the chaos of the "*established global disorder*".

Retabulism and *Dogmatism* [intellectual, religious, aesthetic, artistic, etc.] are the main notions likely to affect an idea, a thought, a proposal, an action, etc. The one [*Retabulism*] using reflection, logic and *pragmatism*, the other [*Dogmatism*] using *conformism*, passion and *Empiricism*. Let us take these "influences" that have managed the world's history as thesis and antithesis; a constantly emerging dialectic. The introduction of new concepts modifying and potentially breaking the hegemony of dogmatism is the basis of the "*supra-logical*" nature, or "*superlogic*" of Retabulism.

For example, in pairs of opposites such as "*Retabulism\falsification*" or "*Retabulism\falsehood*", it is clear that the second term is a psychological concept that the former dissipates. When we introduced the concept of Retabulism, we used an *epistemological* notion, i.e. the strictly real or true concepts methodically sifted from the inaccurate or the false.

Retabulism has meaning only by and for reciprocal relationships with ideas such as knowledge, science, reason, common sense, sensitivity, etc. Even if we stick to a language more concerned with accuracy and logic, that of Retabulism, the fact remains that the will of the individual is an essential variable for the word to have meaning in any real sense. It is from the intelligent and learned mutual relations between men that Retabulism gleans tangible meaning. And it is the consistency of the system of Retabulism, insofar as it is nowhere expressly contradicted by science and reason, that allows us to judge its relevance and effectiveness.

If [Retabulist] relativity is thwarted by the yoke of dogmatism, it can cause humans to become more skeptical. In all areas [historical, theological, sociological, ethical, aesthetic, etc.], a Retabulist proposal makes sense, and is therefore of value in terms of the coordination of a group of men and women, more or less structured and united. Once integrated into this set, Retabulism is effective in maintaining relativity.

- *The relationship between Retabulism and knowledge*

A concept is unambiguously assimilated by Retabulism. Subjecting something to reflection, assessment, and approval gives a proposal Retabulist veracity; its contents, meanwhile, are ideas that seek knowledge.

A first requirement for Retabulism that acquires a categorical or *principal status* is the separation of the false from the true, of error from accuracy, doubt from certainty, of the improbable from the probable, myth from reality, fiction from science, of ignorance from knowledge, and static from dynamic. This is the work of Retabulism!

- *Re-establishing the predefined*

The establishment of an event, of a fact, of a now classic and pre dogmatic history, would not be possible were it opposed to Retabulism [re: if it did not possess reasoning that meets the formal conditions].It is important to consider the relationship between meaning and Retabulism, and we discover that the evolution of the idea of Retabulism, which ensures its normativity thought its rational nature, is inseparable from the acquisition of knowledge. The conditions of the signifier in speech provides Retabulism with its status of improving clarity. When Retabulism argues that global knowledge puts things in their exact place, it occupies a position that acknowledges the existence of the false while rejecting it as nonsense. It therefore stands to reason that Retabulism must terminate the conception that makes ignorance the transitive object of discourse; the conception of false as alternative to absent, of the lie as alternative to silence.

Retabulism must demonstrate the irreducible proposal beyond the choice between predefined speech and tacit silence.

The thesis of Retabulism is inseparable from the demonstration of the possibility of truthful speech. This possibility acts as a logical predicate which asserts knowledge that disengages from ignorance or controversial error in an absolute and definitive way.

Of course, while one may deplore the unconditional advent of *Dogmatism* [intellectual, historical, theological, artistic, etc.], it remains that the very notion, so central to modernism, of Retabulist meaning, would never have existed if the *"historicité"* perpetrated by dogmatic ignorance had not opened the way for the discursive approach of contemporary Retabulist thought.

The thesis of the original essence of Retabulism - certainty in the sphere of logic/knowledge - becomes clear if we take into account the reasonable, the sensible, the observation, exploration, investigation, and brief questioning of the "*commonly accepted*". Indeed, it is in this scheme that, according to Retabulism, the germs of scholarly conceptions of the true or real appear, contrasted with the false or the manufactured—developed in order to deceive, warping the senses.

This concept is intended to restore the phenomenological background of the definition of Retabulism versus a dogmatism that embodies historical falsehood as a modality of contemporary thought. This means that Retabulism is ultimately able to render unquestionable judgment on that which constitutes reality.

Whatever reservations are expressed regarding the anchoring of objective Retabulism as evidence, outside of the effort to guard against *Solipsism*[1], it retains the elements of a true critique of all dogmatic or dogmatizing theory.

---

[1] *Solipsism*. Attitude of the thinking subject that views his or her own consciousness as the only reality; other minds, the outside world, are only representations.

This remains subject to the criteria of Retabulism, of which science and knowledge are the foundation.

These references do not design Retabulism so much as establish the compliance of the characters of its thought with its object: Truth.

The Retabulist views the objectivity of Retabulism as one half of this hermetic relationship.

The Retabulist responds to disinformation and manipulation by seeking clarification of meaning amidst the falsehoods of dogmatism to penetrate to its fundamental structure, its original source. Claiming a form of return to authenticity, Retabulism restores a critical sense of rights that cannot be reduced to a simple theory of knowledge. In fact, Retabulism transcends habit and ignorance and elucidates the possibility of knowledge dynamics resulting in the formation of autonomous logic allowing the individual in which it forms to work more and more in the service of truth.

Thus, the Retabulist declines ignorance, prejudice, and the pre-established - in a word, dogmatism - by shifting focus from the model of imperialist science, to a study of the true, the real, the certain.

Retabulism contests the premise that the historicity of dogmatic discourse is meaningful, since in reality it leads to nonsense, inconsistency if it is subjected to critical reflection. For the rehabilitation of *Truth* [intellectual, religious, historical, ethical, etc.], Retabulism is a timely reminder that a theory of meaning which requires conscious thought is indeed possible with the annihilation of dogmatism [intellectual, philosophical, religious, historical, ethical, ideological, political, etc.].

f - Meaning and Retabulism

Retabulism is characterized as a property of the objective meaningless statement, the logical truth. In other words, a Retabulist proposal [ideological, philosophical, political, historical, religious, etc.] advocating against falsehood endangers dogmatism; which is to say that it challenges as absolute any dogmatism that must speak and be heard first and thus monopolize attention. This is why the Retabulist, particularly interested in the foundations of historical or ideological dogmatic reflection, produces acts of intellectual independence and dynamism.

The Retabulist search for the meaning of true statements, with the help of science and reason, can only take a single path: one that leads to confrontation with dogmatic mystification that clings to a privileged status it views as immutable.

At this point, common sense, science, reason and Retabulism are inseparable because we cannot understand the meaning of a dogmatic statement [whether philosophical, religious, historical, ethical, ideological, political, etc.] without revealing the conditions that demonstrate why it is right or wrong, any more than we can reveal these conditions without clarifying the meaning and true object of the statement.

The criteria of the meaning of Retabulism are that it

regains what has been concealed, tampered with, corrupted or deleted. Thus, Retabulism breaches and plows through all of the rational space left open by negligence or accident to discover reality and restore the truth. This is the situation by which Retabulism can show that it is not reducible to a merely formal concept, but constitutes the structural identity of thought and knowledge [Science, Art, Ethics, etc.]!

Modern Retabulist investigation, logical and/or scholarly, shows that peering beyond apparent, dogmatic statements, reveals structural conditions that provide Retabulism with meaning that, far from ignoring the transcendental dimension of reason, is able to answer the ontological imperative of human society by elucidating global disorder, worldwide chaos. Thus recognized as a predicate attributed to what is sensible, reasonable, insightful, Retabulism will challenge the civilizational definition of truth. Invested with objective meaning, Retabulism acts as substitute for other [relative] truths and leads to a form of realism based on universal values!

- *The test of the significance of Retabulism*

The fact is that all that is recognized as dogmatic in the world must be exposed as uncertain and corrected by Retabulism. Retabulist criticism corresponds to alterations made by dogmatism [intellectual, philosophical, religious, historical, ethical, ideological, political, etc.], and is rendered more problematic by negative requirements presented by, for instance, forgery, or mystification of the truth. Led therefore to revise the initial position of dogmatism, Retabulism gradually liberalizes and discloses its criteria of meaning to forge a clear distinction between the Retabulist statement and the dogmatic statement that will then make it possible to discredit the latter by logical-deductive and factual elements.

A dogmatic statement, for example, "*the Greeks are responsible for the origins of Science and the Muslims were mere imitators*" belongs, according to the Retabulism, to the category of false statement because the intellectual conception of the Greek universe is magical, mythological, superstitious, and by deduction, anti-scientific. Indeed, science is antithetical to magic, mythology, superstition and legend!

This dogmatic statement illustrates a false reductionism which ultimately aims to submit statements to the test of Truth. These statements would then, once manufactured and institutionalized, form an incorrigible and therefore immutable base !

To the first pseudo-historical dogma belongs a dogmatic thesis with a corresponding Retabulist correction, which is actually a Retabulist antithesis. This, the latter, opposes the argument that the artificially prescripted applies only in the context of ignorance, stupidity, disinformation and manipulation. The concept of Retabulism, on which the identity of reflection rests, illuminates cognitive statements inextricably comprised of rational and factual components. The Retabulist process unfolds through criteria and arguments based on scientific laws.

The dogmatic statement "*the Greeks are responsible for Science and the Muslims were mere imitators,*" being an artificial criterion [baseless, counterfeit], is for the Retabulist, an example that serious textual criticism rejects and that is unlikely to be validated by science or reason!

An Empiricism rid of these dogmas amounts to [for Retabulism] a purified vision of scientific knowledge where the ontological problems now agree with those of empirical language, assumed in a comprehensive manner!

Retabulism, developed in the methodological spirit of the empirical sciences, leads to the scientific resolution of the problem of *Dogmatism* on which *Orthodox History*[2] - and its various philosophical or political ideologies - is founded. Does dogmatism not emphasize the aporia of any Retabulist thesis to the very same extent as it puts into question a theory or statement by adducing historical fact?

What makes the statement "*Greece is the home of scholars*" false is not "*Greece*", but that "*Greece is the home of scholars*". It should be noted that the concept of equivocation [or correspondence] used in this type of thesis is defended or imposed by all dogma opposing the sound position that prevails in the Retabulist circuit.

Another strong argument that securely upholds the laws of the Retabulist thesis is that the conception of the true, the authentic, the real, the exact, demonstrates that their reports, considered from an epistemological point of view,

---

[2] *Orthodox history*. History imagined without the Middle Ages compiled, written and circulated during the Renaissance and Enlightenment, and institutionalized and popularized in modern times by the authorities of the Church [and its secular arm]; The history and official historiography of the Christian West.

leads out of the narrow prison of *ignorance-misinformation* and ambivalence adopted by a widespread, traditional dogmatic culture.

Retabulism is committed to maintaining its orientation toward truly empirical knowledge. The Retabulist cannot only refuse to qualify as true or inaccurate that which is revealed as so demonstrated after verification, but must also rely on the concordance of assertions, of facts with the provision of their sources. In a general sense, that which assigns a Retabulist expression its empirical significance is its ability to transcend the true and therefore go beyond the scope of what it *ostensively*[3] indicates.

We cannot situate Retabulists issues outside the field of Knowledge. That said, the Retabulist cannot have a tendency to look for an approximate view that does not consider rectifying its design, its nature, or its origin - by analyzing it in the light of knowledge and reasoning - essential.

Whichever way we turn, it seems that the logic of Retabulism and its correspondence with factual references made in the order of Retabulist knowledge, as many as are made scientifically, sums up to nothing less than the whole of the experience of rational criticism to which the very concept of Retabulism is exposed.

To challenge, threaten, or annihilate a system, doctrine, opinion or referential rule via Retabulism means a victory

---

[3] *Ostensive.* Referring to a proposal to be demonstrated. That which shows what it says, that is its own direct proof.

for knowledge, without compromising understanding, nor returning to thought that is monolithic or arbitrary as that of dogmatism, be it intellectual, ethical, religious, ideological, philosophical, historical, cultural instruction, education-, etc.

This Retabulist priority is relative to understanding [or knowledge] and therefore to that which is made knowable by the tools of Science [Thinking, Observation, Experimentation, Validation, and Modeling] which subscribes to the apprehension of statements, proposals or objects [intellectual, ethical, religious, ideological, philosophical, historical, etc.].

Retabulism is an idealization of what is acceptable within the streamlined operations of science, without reference to passion or emotional state!

- *Pragmatist Retabulism*

Pragmatist inspiration defines Retabulism by success in action and the convergence of ideas that have their source in reflection with a process of questioning that opposes institutionalized dogmas and that which is popularized as true, genuine, real!

Dogmatists thought that nothing would cast doubt on their system [doctrine, history, religion, etc.] and viewed confrontation with facts other than those they fabricated as empirically impossible, but their efforts have proven fundamentally shortsighted.

This simply means that the object of their system, far from claiming a realistic designation, can be challenged on the basis of its questionable structures, which the Retabulist can juxtapose with reality using the tools of Knowledge. Verifiability, a Retabulism concept, coincides with empirical experience.

The idea of idealizing Retabulist objectivity from a methodological standpoint means the possibility of discovering realities other than those usually accepted, and with which we are already familiar. Retabulism recognizes Truth as an irreducible whole, revealed under a universal act of thought. By this Retabulism implies either the gathering of proposals or theses in a set, or the intellectual process by which these are touched on. Retabulism resides internally, in sensible intuition or holistic thinking able to explore all the elements of this intuition. Beforehand, it is necessary to examine the Retabulist thought that intervenes and draws from knowledge while remaining its own scale or measurement.

But Retabulist thought perceives beyond the sphere of reflection. The intellectual act thus rises to discernment, at which point dogmatism reaches its limits and truth reveals itself. Retabulism, conceived of in terms that imply such a formalization is ultimately accountable to the true or Truth.

Does not the idea of absolute Retabulism boil down to a mere sequence of concepts that have a grip on reality? Does Retabulist thought not consist of the reduction of ignorance?

In its disagreement with error, reality manifests in its rationality, as a march to a concrete form of the universal, that is to say, to the [utterly intangible] universal as system, idea, history. Reality, per se, would not allow anything outside of itself. Retabulism is also reflected in the role played by the idea, the sense in which reason and it [Retabulism] are surely inseparable, indeed likely joined in a spirit of continuity. Retabulism can also reveal a hidden side of the non-achievement of humanity that challenges its resistance to the message of reason.

g - Retabulism and its perception

Retabulism emphasizes its irreducibility relative to its perception of the world. Conceptual thought emerges as a logical process is characterized. For the Retabulist, Retabulism is attached to the idea of actual content, independent of thought, reflection. Retabulism thus remains open to all possibilities. It is the integration of sensible aspects that obtain.

When it denies dogmatism[historical, theological, ideological, political, etc.], Retabulism prompts the explosion. With each blast, it immediately reconstitutes in another reflexive, scholarly direction, the process of truth. The world becomes Retabulist on a model erected not on dogma but on absolute principles!

- *Retabulism and Reality*

Retabulism belongs to Universalism, it is not tied to individuals belonging to the same cultural, social, or religious denomination. On the contrary, Retabulism binds to the men and women who make up a history, a space, with its members making up an organism, a language, a human vision of the world. The idea of Retabulism with history as its starting point includes researching historical data, the interpretation of historical facts and the establishment of actions consistent with reason.

Despite its formalism, Retabulism lends an ontological character to its activity that does not go against the faculty of reason. Through the ideas of Retabulism, reason acquires its cognitive value. In line with its rationalist nature, the concept of Retabulism now coincides with the ideal of intelligibility.

Retabulism exercises a regulatory function in historical knowledge because it does not see a gap between reason and truth. Retabulism puts the ontological meaning of dogmatism in check!

By discovering rationality on the same level as events and history and locating the inherent intelligibility of knowledge, Retabulist criticism strongly undermines the idea of dogmatism, falsehood, myth, misinformation, and manipulation!

- *Truth, Retabulism's quests*

Orthodox or absolutist history can be true only if revised and rectified by Retabulism. The real is the natural enemy of the false, refusing to fight the latter and allowing it to grow reduces Retabulism to an abstraction, to nonsense. The fundamental, critical core of Retabulism is its break with the false, with the dogmatic status quo. This includes a categorical imperative to be, while remaining confined to that which is one's own. The Retabulist thought must be thought by its author, without resulting in the imposition or prescription of conditions on others.

The true function of Retabulist thought is not to observe the mess, disorder, lies and immorality but to determine the origins of these, their sources, through a structured, shall we say scientific manner of organization, to isolate, confront, and inevitably, eradicate them. Hence the idea of the historical dimension of Retabulism: history being a key element of the power of dogmatism.

The defense of lies and mystification is only amplified as historiography, culture and more recently media [media, film, Internet, etc.] express the factually inaccurate time and again. Humanity moves toward its own ultimatum: global alienation. Their very nature, biased as it is, calls for their rejection, their denial, concretely effected by the actions of reasonable [re: guided by the universal sense] men, amending nonsense into sense or mining erroneous preestablished givens for what makes rational sense. Therein is the progress to Order, the very movement of history or the dialectical movement of Retabulist thought.

II - Historical and Historiographical Retabulism: a scholarly textual criticism

A - *Definition of Terms*

1 - History

Research, knowledge, and reconstruction of mankind's past in its general aspect or with specific focus; on place, time, or a particular point of view; includes the gathering and assembly of facts.

a - Historian

One who is dedicated to history; relates and analyzes facts and aspects of the past; writes books on history, teaches the discipline.

b - Historiography

The activity of the person who compiled the history of his or earlier times. Books, collections of various written works, as a result of this activity.

2 - The Value of Historiography

In the purview of Retabulism, there are two forms of historiography: *true historiography*, which is very rare, and the *false historiography* that dominates culture. The latter must be assigned to literary critically scientific proposals.

Reflection on *historical Retabulism* does not raise philosophical questions, but scientific ones. First and foremost on its own nature. Two positions - one realistic or marked by truth; the other mythical or marked with falsity - are opposed on this. On one side is *true historiography* or *historiographical Retabulism*. This is defined as the estimation of the historical object in the spirit of science, with the goal of forming an intermediary between logic and said historical object. On the other, *false historiography* or *historiographical dogmatism* is defined either by an accord in the service of manipulation, misdirection, or by a more intrinsically disingenuous character developed to serve an interest.

3 - Historiographical Retabulism

What is the place of historical Retabulism in the History of Human Civilization? Should it eclipse all forms of manipulation on the condition that its judgments on them are true, which is what we expect of it?

Classical Islamic Civilization [*CIC*] is one subject par excellence that studies what is expected of *historical Retabulism*.

4 - Classical Islamic Civilization or CIC [*eighth-fourteenth century*]

a - Definition

"Revolution of all aspects of humanity of a social, religious, moral, aesthetic, technical character, catalyzed by Islam. The evolution of widely-held points of view and currents of thought,

birth of the natural sciences, radical discoveries, revolutionary inventions, a profound transformation of the social order, ethics and economy, which took place in the Muslim empire from the eighth to the fourteenth century that transformed the thinking, ordering, and art of Western society from the ninth to the fifteenth century, generating the Renaissance [XV-XVI century], the modern era[the enlightenment century - XVIII century], and the industrial revolution [XIX century] before its culmination in the contemporary... »

Typically, basic [re: "*classic*" or "*commonly accepted*"] historical propositions are the result of more or less arbitrary political arrangements. This is where historical Retabulism comes in, to put such propositions in their proper place and restore legitimacy to history.

This legitimacy is also reflected in the distinction of the stages through which it is established. We may identify first a stage of very rough historical knowledge belonging to *Classical Islamic Civilization* [*CIC*], flawed and contaminated by falsehood and deliberate disinformation. Then that of scientific or scholarly knowledge of *Classical Islamic Civilization*, minimizing errors.

It is quite common [especially for periods of history earlier than the twentieth century] for stories featuring fictional characters, such as those of the scholars of ancient Greece, to be attributed as history, while evoking intellectual, social and historical facts as *authentic*. Correspondingly, a false historiography is fabricated for CIC, altogether unfavorable, that propagates generally in the leading scholarly sphere that pervades popular culture.

For example, it is true that the founder of inorganic chemistry is Jabir Ibn Hayyan-[Latinized as Geber- 721-815] and that of mathematics is Al-Khwarizmi [Latinized as *Algoritmi* - 800-847], in this sense that which truly demonstrates reason is the measure of *Classical Islamic Civilization*. As the quality of our reasoning improves in terms of *Classical Islamic Civilization*, corresponding progress can be observed in terms of historical Retabulism.

This is true in the sense that there is no proof, outside of *historical dogmatism*, of the existence of Thales [circa 625 - 546 BC] or Hippocrates [circa 569 - 475 BC] or of the supposed "*scientific*" works attributed to them throughout historiography; these figures, if they existed, would have been superstitious, zealous followers of the "magic of mythology". This term is defined as fable, theogony, legend, fable, folklore, anecdote, myth, fiction, utopia, etc. The antonym [term which extends in the opposite direction] of mythology is truth, reality, science, rationality. Therefore, it is consistent with the observations and analysis of historical Retabulism, supported in their own right by Anthropology and Ethnology, to claim that Greek society and, by extension, the ancient Greeks, upheld a culture and universal design that is paradoxical to Science. This implies, finally, that Thales and Hippocrates - were they to exist - could in no way conceive, nor even imagine their alleged works or "*scientific discoveries*"!

Beyond a succession of the stages of reasoning, must we now admit that historical Retabulism ought to challenge dogmatism to restore order to historiography? More than ever according to historical Retabulism, the myth of "*ancient Greece, the cradle of culture and science*" is not only false but meaningless - vitiated as a politico-religious strategy by the ruling classes and Western academia. It was developed in the *Middle Ages*, housed by the *Renaissance*, ordered in *modern times* [*Enlightenment*] and imposed in the eighteenth century, with its heyday in the nineteenth century. Ultimately, it would be accepted as evident in the twentieth/twenty-first century.

Meanwhile, it should be noted that with historical truth, more than elsewhere, historiographical propositions - confound evidence - must fit together perfectly, or else be organized in a system of domination, so that each is consistent with the production of authenticity for those deemed honorable ["*scholars of ancient Greece*", "*ancient Greece, the cradle of culture and science*"] while establishing a lie that can be widely imposed [concerning *Classical Islamic Civilization*].

Basic facts and events elude and change, taking on misleading shades of nuance: for example, CIC and Ancient Greece never carried the same meaning for historical dogmatism!

Through an inverse relationship between *historical dogmatism* and *historical Retabulism*, each acquires meaning, and it is through the meeting of the two systems - in as much as this meeting nowhere expressly contradicts reason and knowledge - that we judge its accuracy. If, through the relative nature of truth, the historical failure of dogmatism is threatened, it will surely lead to changes in historiographical dogmatism, which is its vehicle. In all rational spheres, a dogmatic proposition forfeits its meaning, and consequently becomes a Retabulist constant, so long as it is relative to an incontrovertible contextual whole. But upon integration into such a [Retabulist] set, it is, with respect to the set, true. The Retabulist historical perspective not only relativises dogmatism, but brings about its ruin.

b - Error-proofing Retabulism

There can be no *historical Retabulism* where there is no yearning for truth. If we do not seek historical truth, we do not care about Retabulism. The sanctum of Retabulism, in general and of historical Retabulism in particular, is science.

5 - *Historical Retabulism in popular culture*

Historical Retabulism extends as far as is possible while remaining a critique of the historical dogmatism that is instilled through education and culture. What remedy might be proposed to limit historical dogmatism, be it institutional or of the masses? Against this pseudo-historical illusion do we not discover, through historical Retabulism, remedies against misdirection and deception on a mass scale?

Indeed, historical Retabulism appears not only as an extension of discerning reflection, but also as a break with political and "scholarly" institutional dogmatism. It refers to an experience built on knowledge [Science] and reflection.

6 - *Axiomatic historical Retabulism*

The idea of presenting history axiomatically falls within

the purview of historical Retabulism and is in this respect a model of thought. In fact, in "*classic*" historiographical analyses of *Classical Islamic Civilization* we see that the elements that comprise it clearly played a role in the establishment of institutionalized historical dogma. Hence, historical Retabulism strives to dissolve these artificial representations, attached to such concepts as: "Muslims are imitators of Ancient Greek culture," or "*Muslims are merely the conveyors of Greek science to the West*;" ideas like "*science and culture are naturally western*," "*the West found Greek culture after it disappeared for centuries*," "*Ancient Greece is the cradle of science and democracy*" and the corollaries with which these ideas are associated. Thus formed a strategy that dates back to the Middle Ages, in tandem with an ecclesiastical and secular politics to acquire and translate [into Latin and Greek versions] the comments on culture made by *Classical Islamic Civilization*, repackaged formally with an added monolithic monoscript : *Classical Islamic Civilization* does not/has never exist/ed ! This is what institutionalized *historical dogmatism* has proclaims, a conviction which has prevailed for centuries and which continues to present itself in the scientific world and in that of the masses.

Essentially, *Classical Islamic Civilization* could not result from a religious belief other than Islam, coupled with the work of reason, sensitivity and ken of women and men. This was the idea that was introduced and that has now been presented of *Classical Islamic Civilization*!

In this perspective, the truth is confused with non-contradiction and Retabulism with cohesion. It is thus asked if all historical incongruities could not be reconstructed from logical foundations whose signs and rules are exhaustively laid out and defined. Historical Retabulism may conduct such an undertaking utilizing all historiographical media, which have been refined as standards heightened with time. Indeed, such an endeavor must halt at nothing and cannot shrink from any of the obstacles firmly established by institutionalized *historical dogmatism*.

7 - *Historical Laws of historical Retabulism*

In this light, there exists an explanation of historical events that conforms to reality, which is to say, that adequately represents a set of explainable facts. These center on nature and on causes of historical phenomena, i.e. their effects that are observable, or more accurately, "*reproducible*" in time. This view is etched in the thought of historical Retabulism. Thus, the effects of historical events are subject to a kind of *historical law* or laws that cannot be discovered without rigorous historiographical analysis.

Accordingly, dismantling false historical events is essential. Hence, the attempted explanation of history founded on assumptions that run counter to reality, but also the set of propositions that are not consistent with historical laws.

In light of this discussion, the falsehood of an explanation of historical events can have several causes: the considered historiographical media was chosen arbitrarily; assumptions that express the nature of the historical relationship between limiting variables [original texts, other types of documents, the objectivity of written works, the ethics of the historian or *historiographer*, etc.] were not pertinent or inappropriate; the implementation of verification methods were faulty or nonexistent. Therefore, there can be no comparison of the factual and the counterfeit, of events and non-events, of pieces of documentation with other documentary evidence, of postulates in the process of ongoing investigation.

At the same time, what accords Retabulism its historical laws is a distinctive scientific character, that is, their reproducibility in space and time. They are verifiable and thus refutable; an event or factual premise that is confirmed [logical, rational] will be true, or at worst, acceptable.

With the contention that *Classical Islamic Civilization* served as a foundation [cultural, scientific, socioeconomic, etc.] for Western society, historical Retabulism distinguishes constructive events and the origin of important achievements. The former - as its phrasing suggests - tend, firstly to build representations of the real [observable] such as that of the state of Western society or the quality of life in the Occident before the advent of the *Classical Islamic Civilization*, secondly, the construction of a massive policy of acquisition, translation and reproduction [in Latin and Greek versions] of the works of Muslim thinkers in every existential area [navigational, socioeconomic, transportation, culinary, fashion, nutrition, etc.] in particular that of scholarly thought [Science, Literature, Arts, Poetry, technique, etc.]; the latter, more compromising in its object, takes myth as its fundamental - general, formal - principle, from which we find, deductively, historical laws and facts [operations, works, actions, proceedings, etc.] verifiable by comparison or observation using the tools of the History of the Sciences - ethnological and/or anthropological documents, archaeological materials, linguistic analysis, semantic/lexical studies, etc. All this demonstrates that the fundamental basis of Western society arose from the *Classical Civilization of Islam*.

Consequently, the realization of what is commonly called "*Western civilization*" furnishes proof that undeniably authenticates an origin of the *Civilization of Classical Islam*.

Retabulism produces and recasts intellectual evolution, with profound changes in assumptions, concepts and worldviews that have been established in recent centuries. The idea of evolution appears once the contributions of the *Civilization of Classical Islam* are highlighted in a portrait of history. It is therefore the role of Retabulism to examine Event authenticity within the whole of falsified history.

Retabulism, in an analysis of how history and historiography is perceived by the masses, shows how each of the concepts that we use to see the world result from the simultaneous presence in every individual, in varying proportions, of concepts that shape his - or her - state of mind, opinions, judgments, prejudices, etc.

To avoid the trap of the preconceived, packaged social conditioning, intellectual laziness and the asphyxiation of reason, it is imperative that descriptions of the world be replaced and recovered via reconstruction - both historical and historiographical - so scientific and symbolic operations, through the process of reconstructing facts and events, are made current and exact.

In other words, modeling historical appearances and insisting that they must confront Retabulist assumptions or hypotheses may not be a simple operation but is achievable in a time when the traffic of information is so considerable and once concealed Documents are now accessible. Yet it is appropriate to maintain the designation of hypotheses or scientific proposals of conjecture that exhibit this Retabulist character and are thus provable.

Though this conception of Retabulism in the history of ideas will not always be unanimous, one thing is certain - it loudly proclaims itself to be unworthy of the radical falsification of reality !

In any case, Retabulism remains an effective tool in restoring an actual order of authenticity to the world, far from that of historical and historiographical dogmatism. In other words, does the success of the historical cause of the *Civilization of Classical Islam* really render unthinkable a global resurrection of Truth?

Logical rationality inspires the entire Retabulist endeavor but succeeds only when it accepts a definitive break with pre-established dogmatism, when it values how history is perceived, and with a firm sense of being an individual who reasons !

8 - Retabulism and the likelihood of facts

In the above, the fact that we may track and manage the elements that establish historical facts to highlight the possible falsity of a statement is implicitly granted. In history, in most cases, the conditions under which truth is prospected are tough: [due to] missing vestigial evidence; flaws in the supporting documents, written testimony, etc. Therefore, determining whether an event actually occurred must be done carefully. The forms of Retabulism are twofold in this respect ; *theoretical and practical.*

Consider the likelihood of an event: an initial examination reveals various indications that, most of the time, do not uniquely evidence the defined event. The problem of authenticity or factual likelihood will be, for additional tests, to check various assumptions and, wherever possible, to confer a status of validity, truth, or at least a high degree of probability.

When the circumstances of historical fact are reconstituted based on evidence and/or fictional stories, one encounters difficulty because we cannot reproduce the past; the investigation can only go back to the probable or reasonable causes, especially since a single historical record - an illustration on a ceramic piece, for example - can be interpreted in various ways and thus lead to different conclusions.

For example, every vestige of historical evidence [vases, utensils, prints, etc.] discovered during archaeological excavations in Egypt is regarded by Egyptologists as funereal. Egyptology goes on to allow the physicist, the chemist, the anthropologist, the architect, etc. to give their respective views on these findings.

Scientifically, it is generally more difficult to go from

effects to causes than to predict the effects of an event when the laws governing similar phenomena and their initial conditions are known. When a statement or a historical proposition concerns the past, the determination of cause and effect cannot be asserted without documents, relics, monuments, testimonials, etc. from other sources. In such a case, what endures of the past remains, unfortunately, a reference. It follows that Retabulism cannot accord Science and History the same level/status since the Human take on the past [re: history] is less certain than on infinitely reproducible scientific experiments. The fabrication of Greek antiquity[the Classics] by humanists in the fifteenth and sixteenth century remains thus a clear example of the influence of man's historiographical arsenal [print, painting, sculpture, architecture, engraving, etc.] on history for ulterior ends, characteristic of schematics which can be described as anti-historical.

The ethical code of historical professionals is, "Better to have anything, true or not, with which history may be erected, than to have nothing at all." For the Retabulist, however: "it is better to have no way of substantiating history than to make use of the false"!

9 - Epistemological Design of Retabulism

Retabulism easily identifies truth as it relates to finite differences, in consecutive improbabilities of a fact or historical events. Retabulism is consistent with a conception of Truth that aligns with reflection and with a reality that involves comparing current knowledge with actuality, which of course is not readily available but requires a long process of investigation, off the beaten course.

To apprehend it, science is the great tool that provides methods to weigh against each other to evaluate which will lend themselves to the authentication of facts or historical events and which to refutation. In a word, a [Retabulist] epistemological and differential opinion or stance does not need to be operative and full of a metaphysical conception of truth. However, it is undeniable that when Retabulism corrects a historical fact we near, hence, Truth.

Retabulism is interested in anything that has to do with what has happened: whether as a chain of events, or the recounting of this sequence of facts or events. Therefore, Retabulism highlights a narrative of facts and real events, as opposed to a chronicle or romantic saga. By this standard of authenticity, Retabulism proves itself to be methodologically similar in some ways to science; as an action or a process of knowledge.

Of course, it is not comparable from a fundamental point of view to scientific disciplines such as physics or molecular biology. Indeed, Retabulism is a knowledge of events, whereas science is a knowledge of the laws governing the facts.

a - Retabulism: the intellectualist activity

Retabulism is interested in understanding both the singularity of events, and their specificity, i.e. [that which is intelligible of] what they offer. The Retabulist has to hold himself to a standard of unselfishness, as opposed to a mere storyteller, or a propagandist or a nationalist or civil service historian. The strictly intellectual character of historical knowledge - for Retabulism - represents a venture driven by the love of truth and a simple curiosity to verify the authenticity of facts and historical events set up as dogma.

Nothing that is historical is foreign to Retabulism. It must be kept firmly in mind that the vision we have of the past is rarely presented by history and historiography. By correcting this through Retabulism, we increase our dignity - that which commands the respect of another. Indeed, this includes the sort of objective statements that comprise authentic historical knowledge.

It is to misunderstand *dogmatic historiography* and *Orthodox history* in general, not to see that they are often a sum of norms and traditions that set a social dimension: National and dynastic memories, collective myths, folklore, legends, etc. To equate such manufactured [re: fabricated] national and ethnic narratives with scientific history is to confuse the essence of a thing with its origin. In a way, this is no different from distinguishing medicine from quackery, chemistry from magic.

A Retabulist seeking knowledge[of unadulterated truth] unselfishly limits his vision of the world to the refutation of collective myths on which contemporary history is founded. Retabulism has no right to ignore that the foundation on which contemporary history has for centuries reposed rests on knowledge that is only somewhat objective. *The Culture of the Classical Islam*, which is a projection of the past and present of Western society, was recast by the West in a Eurocentric and anti-intellectual historiography.

b - Sociology of Retabulism

The object of Retabulism - History - is intimately linked to the relationship between knowledge and society. Therefore, it focuses on the observation of public opinion and popular beliefs; Such as the dissemination of historical knowledge in the public, for example.

Indeed, Retabulism is a passage, a "*recovery*" of the explanation of history which consists of an emancipation of the collective consciousness of dogmatic or "*orthodox*" historiography or "*official*". As such, sociological implications are what would be responsible for a deviation of thought mired in false mythical explanations and for causes being invented rather than sought after, so only Retabulist thought, truly free from institutional and/or social conditioning, can reach the truth.

Retabulism indicates that the early stages of rational thought produce concepts, attitudes, etc. that recognize that knowledge is not true merely because its origin is social. Retabulism asserts that society introduces subjective elements in its construction of history. But this relativism will subside as collective consciousness becomes proficient in Retabulism.

Ultimately, the company of Retabulism, becoming properly conscious and rational, will lead therefore to a truly objective Retabulism. Finally, the progress of Retabulism, being linked to that of society, is foundational of a growing base of knowledge for the well-being of humanity as well as its validity.

However, we must remember some important lessons. On the one hand, Retabulism has in fact demonstrated that the forms and categories of historical facts and events may vary considerably across societies. Here the importance of the sociological variable manifests with the most proof: for each type of society, a method of Retabulism; this would lead to a broad pluralism in favor of history. The nature of the relationship between a social framework and Retabulism depends on whether the individuals who compose it are intellectually conscious; aware of their being manipulated.

- *Retabulism and the dissemination of knowledge*

Retabulism stresses the importance of communication in the development of thought and also, lastly, the fact that the progress of knowledge can be conceived only through the Truth and the authentic distribution of truth. The object of Retabulism might be described as avant-garde; the empirical courses of study that open before it are vast in scope and number. Two main lines are worth retaining: *Retabulism in education*, particularly that of the teaching of history, which will try to reconsider the functions of historians and the official history of academia and its effects.

On the other hand, *Retabulism in communication* is concerned about the effects of audio-visual means of dissemination of dogmatic historiography. Retabulism goes so far as to support calling into question the entire cultural system of our civilization: the devastating effects of mass media on culture which is nothing less than media poisoning or, in other words, acculturation. Changes that occur in all cultural groups [concerning how to act, perceive, judge, work, think, speak, etc.] as a result of continuous contact with an arsenal of means of communication [TV, radio, cinema, internet, books, magazines, newspapers, etc.] appertain to a politico-financial consortium whose plans for Humanity are real.

Retabulism overcomes philosophical presuppositions and epistemological ambitions controlled or unbridled, by moving towards the search for functional correlations between different types of distribution of the truth, to obtain authentic knowledge, defined appropriately. A plethora of perspectives remain open.

Retabulism operates on the level of pragmatic spirit, it transports the mind, as it illuminates the truth. But the idea of Retabulism draws its true fulfillment from putting into place the pieces of existence. From randomness, man passes to the reasonable, to the universal. Such a movement towards the concrete, that is to say towards the achievement of freedom occurs in a world that, if it reflected, would be the world of autonomy, of intrinsic rights.

Tradition is the custodian of the very most inappropriate expressions, appearing from custom by a kind of natural selection. These expressions support distant utopian goals and merely shirk the explanation of unverifiable statements and particular experiences, and are therefore chimerical. Furthermore, Tradition is a common language which maintains existence in ignorance or naiveté because it has not been reformulated to meet the requirements and models of Science.

The contributions of theological Retabulism cover

traditionalist discursive acts [in intention and action] in which argument is based. The submission of action to traditionalist standards accords senselessness to human action, by appending action to rituals of all kind. Whatever the social, economic or cultural conditions, these actions place a value on each individual in the face of an implicitly constituted, organized traditionalist power.

A theology of reality assumes the appearance of an ontological questioning of a different order than what is usual or customary. This very real riddle realizes the freedom of the individual and her or his overall development. It is this question that puts every human in relation with others, along with standards and institutions. Ultimately, towards theological Retabulism this issue courses.

III - Theological Retabulism

Theological Retabulism is the scientific presentation of theological themes so as to characterize unambiguously the articulation and rules of admissible evidence. In any case, the importance of Retabulism - in the modern, scientific sense - boils down to phrasing.

Theological Retabulism is linked to the development of axiomatic expressions, and the study of various sorts of - typically multivalent - concrete structures in the Universe, present in the most diverse spheres of nature.

In other words, knowledge of God can be found on the primary screen of, say, *a high-resolution electron microscope*[4], observing organic tissue or a human cell; or in the eyepiece of a telescope while studying a constellation. In this sense, the work of Retabulism is done within a formalized language; we could say that it highlights the formal character of theological knowledge.

---

[4] The high technical level of high-resolution microscopes allows the viewing of macromolecular biological structures on the nano [even pseudo-atomic] scale to obtain their three-dimensional structure such as cellular and viral protein complexes, ribosomes, wrapped viruses, etc.; as well as visualization of biological objects such as mitochondria, parts of a cell, irregular viruses, etc., by means of electron tomography. This imaging technique endeavors the reconstruction of the shape of a single object from a series of measurements made at different angles, similar to the medical scanner, but on the molecular level.

A - The Idea of Formal Theological Retabulist Knowledge

The idea of a formal Theology of Retabulism is, in a sense, as elementary as a scientific mode of reflection. The views expressed in a formal theology of Retabulism reduce thereby the meaning of Traditionalist concepts to the rules of their use, distinguishing it from mere interpretation, or representation, relegated to the status of custom.

In this analysis of *theological Retabulism*, the [inaccurately labeled as] "Islamic" *Tradition*[5] is an excellent model of analysis and observation, as an exemplar of

---

[5] *Tradition* [*Hadith*]: Means an oral communication, words supposed to have been uttered, and the actions alleged to have been carried out by Mohammed, the transmitter of the message of Islam. In the 10th and 11th century, these alleged statements were compiled in book form [Bukhari & Muslim, Al-Nawawi, etc.] and served as an opportunity for each consecutive generation of *saint*, *spiritual "guide"*, *religious leader*, *Imam*, or *Traditionnist* [*or Hadithist*] to complete it with additions. Like the *Talmud* these collections include all of what is called *Tradition* that purports to be related to the actions and words of Mohammed and his companions. This *Tradition* was originally imposed in the 14th century by socio-political [*Kaliphs, Viziers, Sultans*, etc.] and spiritual [*Imams, Oulémas, Muftis*, etc.] authorities, enforced under penalty of, on the one hand, a divine curse; and on the other, sanctions for disobedience, as principles of both a personal and collective governance for Muslims. The *hadiths* were reported by tens of thousands of companions [Ismail Ibn Kathir, "As-Sira". Edit. Universal, 2007, p.927]. Cf. "Annex - *Hadith*".

reflection [like the *Talmud*[6], or the *Gospels*[7] and *Christian hagiology*[8]]. In this sense, [theological] Retabulism appears as the capacity to create rational objects: explanations -while defining a theological structure according to scientific critiques: discerning theological variables beyond the sphere of extravagant speculation, replacing the [de facto] illogical with logic, what is unintelligible with the intelligible, the irrational with the rational, in short, the false with truth.

1 - Retabulism and Theological Liberation

Suspicion and critique carried out by the developing Retabulist movement, originating in deep contemplation of monoscripts ; monolithic historical and historiographical objects and methods.

The singularity of theological Retabulism is that it promotes a sincere interest in the question of metaphysical truth. It sets to work illuminating and reformulating the mandates of a theological, cultural, social, and political order that oppresses the *Tradition*.

The variety of the situations and problems perpetrated by the Tradition are characterized on the one hand by a zombifying tone and on the other by an intense, paralyzing anxiety, cultivated like a religious doctrine.

---

[6] *Talmud*. Oral law [or *oral Torah*]. It consists of all recollections of substance, in particular those constituting the code of *Michna* and its commentary [Palestinian or Babylonian], *the Guemara*.

[7] *Gospels*. Literally "*Good News*". The profession of salvation for all offered in Jesus Christ. And, by extension, the life and teachings of Christ by the Apostles, foundational of the Christian faith.

[8] *Hagiology*. Recollections or sets of recollections dealing with the Saints and the Saintly.

Theological Retabulism focuses on cultural issues, especially contemporary unbelief or religious extremism, while maintaining sensitivity to cultural, socio-economic and political factors at the root of these. Theological Retabulism advocates first the logic of rational action, and second an emancipatory praxeology[9] that goes well beyond a defense of the individual or the rights of man [i.e. human rights, in an exclusively theoretical sense].

Retabulism situates theological discourse on a specific object: God, the universe, the individual, confidence, spiritual life, etc. - to which it grants decisive relevance. Tradition, meanwhile, takes the perspective of a doctrine of salvation: an archaic and outdated discourse, inattentive to the concrete, historical and political conditions of the individual today.

Tradition exhorts its object of faith, a mysterious and Almighty God outside history and outside of Humanity!

The main theme of theological Retabulism is freedom and just action, in the light of knowledge [for which science is the principal vector]. It takes over Traditionalist Orthodoxy, that is, virtuous thought on what is absurd, aberrant. Due to the innovative nature of its approach on objects of *certitude*[10] Retabulism is defined as resolutely

---

[9] *Praxeology*. Science or theory of action ; knowledge of the laws of human action which lead to operational conclusions [operational research, cybernetics, etc.].

[10] The term "*faith*" is inappropriate and nonsensical, we prefer the term "certainty;" much more adequate and in accord with the scientific approach. Indeed, in Science, there is certainty - of a valid observation, analysis, and experiment.

practical, applied knowledge, in that it starts from the analysis of reality and action within which it is circumscribed. Hence, it encounters practical science, intending to experience the world rather than dream it. In this regard, the Tradition has a separate position on the issue; one which refers to this or that element of doctrinal theory, to any ritual instrument of its "*religious*" arsenal.

Tradition [and "*religious*" and philosophical sectarian currents] warns its followers, as well as all those who do not adhere to its doctrine, of the potential for misinterpretation with respect to the official deity. Some have understood that to deepen reflection on the Retabulist movement they must drive their own personal crusade [intellectual, rational, moral, emotional, behavioral, etc.] to observe the outright condemnation of a pernicious Tradition.

a - The Tradition: A Rebellion against Reason

Oh how woeful the phenomenon of human history to which the Tradition refers! The obsession with power that led to its creation overstepped the bounds of the strictly "*religious*" to invest in the private, socio-economic, political, and cultural spheres, thereby changing the face of human society to its collective disadvantage. Because the Tradition implies a relationship of power with *supratheology*, its original course is in conflict with that of Science and its discerning. A diversity of doctrinal currents generated by the teaching it establishes and imposes have been employed by authorities of Traditionalism to exclude enlightened thinkers, accusing them of apostasy and deception.

The grievance that is Tradition has unleashed at different times and places various measures of intolerance, prohibition, exclusion and removal - by means of pseudo-religious operations and procedures.

Theological Retabulism reveals the inferiority of Tradition through cognitive language because it [cognitive language] keeps track of the customs of ignorance, and meets the most acute form of intellectual contempt. In the history of religions, the Tradition is applicable - by analogy - to the primitive period of Humanity!

The Tradition played a significant role in the destruction which led to the irretrievable ruin, for example, of the *Civilization of Classical Islam*. At a time when all Muslim society was marked by *supratheology*, messages and/or doctrinal propositions revealed humanity's most fundamental aspirations and thus had, inevitably, cultural, scientific, socio-economic, and, naturally, political consequences.

Without adopting a simplistic model that would whitewash the adverse metamorphoses caused by Tradition and instead credit social factors, Retabulism demonstrates their influence to better understand their power and effects. From its onset in the XI-XII century, the Traditionalist crisis that shook the Muslim Empire had all the traits of a corrosive and authoritarian "*socio-religious*" movement.

Most Traditionalist currents have popular origins and are rooted in the expression of organized social resentment, fed and disseminated by the sectarianism of the proponents of Tradition!

The Tradition and a good number of its sectarian movements want to reform Theology and the world - in the image of mass stupidity, poverty, intolerance, and violence - by producing utopias that mobilize the energies of the faithful. With no ideals to defend and no cause to triumph, and its civilizational projects nonexistent, the main action of the unofficial [formal] Tradition is often violent; futility, ritualization of individual actions, glorification of the *Fathers of Tradition* and the sacred, instrumentalization of fear of the people - these are the means by which it does combat with *Knowledge* and *Civilization*. Simply quote the painful *Spanish Inquisition* and fatal seizure of the power of the *Khaliphal* organized by the Ottomans; recall the widespread colonization of the Muslim lands; recall thus the involvement of Tradition and the spoils it managed to reap.

Given its pluriform reality, the Tradition has been, at one time or another, the pseudo-religious challenge, innovation, and reaction - it has used and abused pseudo-claims of a social character, pseudo-dissent of an ethnic character, and pseudo-resistance of a nationalist one in the creation of a new *anti-theological* belief. Its sole concern: the draw of power, submission of the people to its doctrine and its rituals, toward the overall loss of cultural identity and finally, the abolition of the most elementary rights of the individual [freedom of thought, movement, etc.]. Theological Retabulism highlights the conflict in which Tradition played instigator, and for which it offered so many excuses - for its role in the proliferation of wrath and disorder throughout the centuries of human history [that continues to this day]. Further, the conceptual systems and rituals Tradition produced are among the most vicious and harmful to the human mind, as is allegedly religious speculation which continues to dominate and direct the existence of countless people.

The Tradition was not without effects, whether in culture, aesthetics or human sensitivity, yet it remains indifferent!

2 - The Axiom of Theological Retabulism

The evolution of theological understanding converges with the development of axioms, that is, knowledge considered axiomatic, which issues mainly from ontological reflection on the part of humanity. All Retabulism requires to grant it license to consider the field of theological objects is logical consistency in the relationships that define it in part implicitly.

Similarly, Retabulism shows that the meaning of theological propositions in no way contradicts the consistency of the axiomatic system of the universe. Here, understanding of why Retabulism is not just a means of praxeological expression, but tends to turn into the object of metaphysical inquiry and genuine critical experimentation is even better!

The Retabulist project of metaphysical reasoning and the construction of a theological discourse is not opposed to logic. On the contrary, by logical conclusion it is a set of notions considered to be universal, by virtue of being - by rational thought - intelligible a priori, and inseparable from their meaning. Conceptions of divinity, physical laws of immanence, rationality, evidence, proof, etc. - of all that which is sound - such are the examples of these universal notions. According to Retabulism, the theological approach's fundamental issue [i.e. the issue of its foundation] is the construction of an explicit logical definition of the divine that substantiates its content of purely logical meaning.

The example of the cell observed under an electron microscope or constellation seen through a telescope illuminates the patently fundamental problem of understanding the divine, since the methods of investigation originate in the emotional, the imagination, dreams and so allow God to enter into the real. Therefore, all notions of accessing these by traditional or dogmatic forms, so forms of Tradition, are equivalent to misunderstanding, delusion, or ignorance. The construction of intelligible systems or theological discernment, the historical origin of which we saw can be sought in the humanities, will thus determine reflection of larger epistemological interest. With Retabulism, logical concepts which are practiced implicitly and/or explicitly in the theological work correspond initially to the objective of foundational metaphysics, which is very clear from the perspective of the *logicist*[11]. These concepts respond to the idea of change in the object of theological logic by discernment. Therefore, deep is the break with a representation of Tradition because Retabulism excludes the imaginary reference - at least on an *operative*[12] level. The

---

[11] *Logicist*. Attitude of mind characterized by focus on laws of logics as to apply them to areas outside logic. Endeavor to oppose the methods of logic and psychology.

[12] *Operative*. Regarding a methodically order and operation ; which can be used in an operation led by logic.

phantasmagoria, the fabulous tale, is rejected in favor of the obvious logical concepts, shall we say, the scientific ones, that excite with the powers of insight in this regard.

Retabulism certifies that the only way to understand theology and exegesis is to use the light of Science!

A simple formal scientific system can be used to reveal the logic of theological propositions. The logical operations which it performs leads to metaphysical certainty. The introduction of specific axioms [e.g. the laws of physics] evidence in this manner the logical nature and the authenticity of the concepts [re: truths] in a metaphysical demonstration !

We can also say that Retabulism establishes such unification, which illustrates the true historical relationship of logic and theology outside the realm of the Tradition, which contaminates it.

The logic of Retabulism endorses progress and the understanding of the historicity of a fact or event as much as its theological or *historical-theological* applications, and overhangs from up high the universal validity, the patently a priori [of a fact or event]. Theological Retabulism represents an aspect of the work of Science, which totally supports it.

3 - The Logical-Theological Notion of Retabulism

This does not mean that a rigorous way does not exist to distinguish between logical axioms and theological propositions.

This discernment is a matter of interpreting an intellectual *system*[13], that is to say, constructing a model or way of reasoning, a set of theological objects that can be correlated to the parameters or elements of the scientific system. In fact, the object of theoretical theological logic is found to be completely removed from abstraction and situated on a systemic [related to a system or that which acts on a system] level, by a movement Retabulism calls *systemation*, which poses as new the concept of coherence or logic where theological knowledge is expressed.

The concept of the logico-theological - with its problems, if not its objectives - identifies with what Retabulism calls *supratheology* that is to say: "*a theology that lies in understanding a field of physical sciences by physical means, to understand the laws of nature such as science understands them or may one day understand them*".

In any case, supratheology can provide a formalized scientific knowledge of the neglected objects which are facts and theological events that once existed under the rule of theologians tormented by ignorance, obsessed with the irrational, magical, and indiscernible.

Among the most remarkable results of the classical theological discourse or tradition, and those that best illustrate its absurdity, are the formally absurd themes, the so-called *dumbing down* of society. The most famous of these is an attribution of knowledge of the divine to archaic

---

[13] *System*. Construction of a mindset of proposals, principles and conclusions which form a body of doctrine; a coherent theoretical construction, which accounts for a large set of phenomena.

figures, who allegedly had been instilled with knowledge because they felt they were close to the arrival of a revelation or divine message [re: the Apostles, Companions, Disciples]. Retabulism outlines the formalized absurdity, which is to say, the commitment to build a traditionalist interpretation of the original formal theological system into which figures the proposal of a pseudo-theological formal system of tranquilization that is represented by the Tradition. This latter claim is formally improvable by Science [the laws of physics or nature]. Of course, construction of such teachings exclude the possibility of a demonstrable formula that any interpretation of an authentic or real proposal would fit into. The condition sine qua non of the Tradition is its sum of absurdities and nonsense belonging to a pre-scientific - and thus irrational - era.

The attempt to represent the truth of theological propositions through absurdity no longer has coherent meaning!

What is the meaning we are dealing with here? That which accompanies formalized vegetation? Theological Retabulism shows that the semantic notion of truth [which makes sense only for an interpretation of the original formal theological system] highlights the purely logical or scientific notion of demonstrability. And, since the interpretation of an original formal theological system is controlled by the logical properties of the system itself, the logic of the system allows that the notion of truth, which it is able to characterize exactly [to the degree of the progress of Science] be defined. From the perspective of the idealist, the work of Retabulism is a victory for scientific and theological thought, which explains the Science of Theology, a sort of intellectual symbiosis: Physical evidence to substantiate metaphysics and vice versa!

Retabulism provides support to the development of a logic of theology with the wisdom of the finitude of human knowledge, freed from the yoke of the infamous Tradition !

How can one access divinity if the mind is frozen in complacency ?

4 - Retabulism and Theological Knowledge

Retabulism highlights the realization made through theology of the notion of formal knowledge. As a movement characteristic of the work of Science, Retabulism here concerns a problem more traditionally staked out by philosophy.

If *Traditionalists* or the *historical Keepers of Tradition* come to define themselves as holders of a formal order of knowledge, Retabulism will obviously refute their claim to such knowledge.

The question may arise relative to Science, where the Tradition [classical theology] is commonly considered only as a discourse lacking argumentative consistency, applied to the construction of utopian models of material reality and adapted to an ignorant or gullible public.

Retabulism actually poses, to the epistemology of Tradition, the question of its relationship with [experimental] Science with the demonstration of its constitutive role generating new ignorance as its end.

This is why the illogical Tradition must be submitted to scrutiny from a combination of rigorous technical and scientific concepts and empirical observations. Its supratheological investigation is thereby able to conduct a systematic deconstruction to destroy this still alive and kicking archaic dogmatism : *Tradition*.

Retabulist reason and common sense reveal - in the contradictions in the usage of the Tradition, in the multiplicity of its rituals and the harm wrought upon language by its aberrant practices - the very condition of its stupidity. Therefore, the application of Retabulism is not only its ability to provide insurance in consistency, but also its eliciting of internal doubts in the consciousness of the individual. And so we see in a Retabulist thought, insight, or rather, a lucidity of mind able to confront the demons of Tradition to the degree of acquisition of knowledge development.

Retabulism puts the content of the Tradition to the test by bringing scientific argumentation to bear against it, excluding de facto any false position. Faced with the uncertainty of the dogmatic designations of Tradition, Retabulism draws attention to the extent of the errors, and disasters it occasions - which cover a wide range of existential domains - all while portraying itself as "*open* [*to listening*]" and "*near*" to the individual for the "salvation" of his or her soul.

Retabulism examines the truth and falsehood of the proposals of Tradition in their relation to an understanding of the divine. In other words, Retabulism presents, unambiguously, the semantic contents [whether temporal or modal] intelligible in terms of belief and knowledge.

Retabulism is interested in the history of theology that blends with tradition. So far, in fact, the idea that the Tradition is inseparable from religious belief [or theology] has prevailed, its history being essentially closed and complete. A renaissance of the Tradition in contemporary times has helped to place it in historical perspective of practical meaning, with salutary implications for its disciples; it so offers them the prospect of evolution in their understanding of the divine, of the victory of spiritual over material; of *Metaphysical ideation over a systematization of Physics.*

5 - Analytical Retabulism

The Retabulist perception of the universe is encompassed by science that aims to explore all the activities at work in the construction, development, and dissemination of the Tradition [or other religious currents].

A Retabulism of theological order exposes, in its broad strokes, the presentation of knowledge within the Tradition and religious currents [sects, orders, etc.]. But, first, Retabulism transforms the Traditionalist design of pseudo-religious objects [rituals, habits, uses, and customs; clothing, food, behaviors, etc.]. At its base we find the concept of self-knowledge or freedom of action, of movement, expression. Retabulism is not a theory of philosophical judgment, rather, it is formal knowledge of the relevance of genuine, sound proposals to the relationship between the divine, the human, and fictitious representations, inaccurately fomented by Tradition. The proposals of Retabulism do not result from abstraction, they are entities that have real existence in space or time. These make up the intelligibility of divine concepts, far and removed from the subterfuge, general anaesthetizing, and ignorance of Tradition.

Retabulism puts all knowledge - be it subjective, human, divine, or otherwise; any judgment or privileged claim - in service of Humanity!

Proposals considered Traditionalist [or of Tradition] are often divided into an infinite regression. It is in this range of demonstrations that Retabulism was inspired to demonstrate the existence of an infinite set of nonsense. Unlike the Traditionalist doctrine that prioritizes the abstractions of the unverifiable, the improbable and defines the Traditionalist statement as a combination of sound ideas or concepts; revelations [by God]. This view allows Retabulism to define antitheses easily, with the added support of indisputable argumentation.

To achieve a concept of truth, Retabulism goes through the *analytic*[14] stage. A statement can be said to be analytic if it contains at least one signification, so that all variable substitutions create statements with the same truth value.

In other words, either all Traditionalist claims are true, or they are all false. The analytical property validates Retabulist truth; coinciding with the notion of authenticity, and generating only true, anti-Traditionalist propositions.

---

[14] *Analytic*. Related to, relative to, analysis, that which proceeds from analysis.

6 - *The Epistemo-Retabulist Aspect*

A theological proposition is designated as *true* if it has been established by critical methods, if it is the subject of scientification. A belief in the truth of a proposition or statement, be it scientific or theological, is supposed to result from objective procedures: all evidence prompts assent and trust given these procedures, which in turn point to another belief: *certainty*.

Retabulism examines these issues in relation to the notion of truth, with canonical requirements for evidence and retaining, as essential, that its criteria are found to be accessible. There cannot be any lack of evidence or any evidence that would be fundamentally unverifiable. For example, awareness of the existence of the divine is provable in an indirect and absolute manner-simply observe nature, life; for the still more skeptical, but consider the complexity of matter through a high-resolution electron [or transmission or even photon] microscope. Any problematic notions such as chance, accident, luck, probability, or otherwise random sequences of events that claim to be ontological [the materialization of life, the soul, death, the divine, etc.] have no sense. The Retabulist objects to wanting to dispense with the notions of fact, empirical testing, or truth.

a - The proposal and the fact

For a theological assertion to correspond to the facts or reality, the elucidation of this rapport is the task of Retabulism. The concept of theological truth, for

Retabulism, is a repositioning of the problem in the sense that it ought to agree with the facts.

We say therefore that a theological proposition is true if it achieves satisfaction of all the objects of science and reason and false otherwise. Thus, if we take the proposition "Man was created ex nihilo [out of nothing] and is not a fruit of chance nor of genetic mutations," the truth condition of this proposal is consistent with facts that reasoning and science can easily prove.

Scientifically, there is no correspondence between man and any other creature on Earth, making him [man] the consequence of an act of a *Supreme Intelligence* [God] for a specific purpose. For the statement "Man is an entity that arises on earth according to a decision at a particular time, for a given period of time, according to a given purpose" to be true equates to simply asserting, for example, that the Qur'an reveals and develops this proposition throughout its verses. Hence, the Qur'an meets *supratheological* requirements.

However, there may be an objection on the part of unbelievers, in whom the angle of aperture of consciousness is narrowed or closed due to reflective deficiency, lack of knowledge or simple intellectual limitation. This is an insurmountable obstacle that Retabulism allows us to bypass by means of its logical-deductive elucidation, made possible when we deign to actually understand the truth of a theological proposition and not confuse it with a Traditionalist proposition.

Therefore, the analysis of the proposition and of this fact remains whole and its empirical value retains its import. This is perhaps the final signification of so-called Retabulist epistemologies.

Such intellectualization of theological phenomena can be beneficial only for the development of knowledge, while permitting the release of a perennial and sterile antagonism, between Science and Theology - between the retainers of Metaphysics and those of Physics !

b - Evidentiary Devices

The theological proposal and empirical fact prove to be the *principle*[15] merits of the intelligible. For the Retabulist observer, scientific proposals occur within the limits of the criteria of rational validity [natural laws], which exist as coherence of the whole, and in the face of a proposition [traditionalist, historical, or historiographical] that opposes this set of laws or its protocols, the Retabulist will decide on whether to validate or reject them. Like historical and historiographical dogmatism, it is necessary that the form of Traditionalist or pseudo-theological dogmatism, which is an arbitrary system that chooses to pose as empirically established. Absurdity and skepticism can only identify thus from afar and thereby mislead man, ossifying thought and freezing reason.

The absence of the principles of empirical methodology [objective reasoning] in the Tradition is evidence in a *strict*

---

[15] *Principle.* As in the primary cause.

sense that attests to its being too embarrassed to announce itself as credible and truthful. More, the Tradition represents a model that, due to its absurdity, has long failed to meet the expectations of humanity, which wants only than to rid itself of Tradition's malevolent influence and to emancipate itself to the advantage of experiment. This constitutes the work of technologies that originate in scientific theories committed to accessing objects of a conceptual and historico-theological background. Corroboration of theological data comes from the assumptions or theories from disciplines such as anthropology, sociology, ethnology, archeology, etc., implying such facts independently prove the [theological] data.

c - Proof and Justification

A scientific review shows that the evidence of a Traditionalist proposal is only one aspect of the dislocation of the sets of problems or paradoxes it settles. In terms of Retabulist knowledge, this means that the real issues are upstream [at the origin, source] of Traditionalist genesis, i.e. in an explanation of Traditionalism, with elucidated inherency. Retabulism is invested in sticking to a coherent whole, relying on inconsistencies in Traditionalist data to reveal its contradictions with explanations of scientific validity [anthropological, archaeological, etc.].

In epistemo-Retabulist terms, the primacy of theological evidence is that its propositions come from different areas of knowledge, accrediting its veracity!

Retabulism presents the intellectual aspects of a

theological problem of which the metaphysical dimension is expressed in the concepts of freedom, choice, free will, and responsibility. Analysis of Retabulism should thus start with an overview of the cultural contexts into which the concept has been inserted to clarify and isolate the nexus of Traditionalist contamination. It is through a psychological or psychoanalytical approach that the problem can be identified and confirmed.

Retabulism is primarily rooted in the vitality of the authentic, its energy powers the motivations of human action, and thirst for truth; Retabulism participates in a rationality that, by joining the quest for knowledge and desire to discover, becomes practical reason, as distinguished from the chaos of Tradition. We too can seize the opportunity to quest for intellectualism, enlightened by rational motives.

7 - *The critical context*

With Retabulism the conditions of reflexive certainty appear which allows speaking on an inner ontological experience [liberty, the unseen, the unknown, etc.]. Critical Retabulism ensures that only objective knowledge is accorded to the order of theology, giving it intelligible, human, shall we say emotional, meaning, as opposed to solely material, devoid of emotion. The result is that man can know his nature only as a function of the laws of causality.

The way out of rationalism is in the fallacy of Tradition, which is a figure of the Transcendentalist illusion, that is, of the fundamental error which metaphysics has to this day been sealed without being able to extirpate itself.

The Koran in its initial state of universal message, for example, clearly remains, above all, a tool for reflection a "*garde-fou*", i.e. an exit that allows access to freedom or prevention of falling into the abject, error, mischief, the inaccurate, falsehood, inauthenticity, the infamous; a tool which prevents the calamity of irrational Tradition, and any attempt by it to constitute its hold on the individual, society, memory and history.

Does this mean that a critical Retabulist will succeed in eliminating all traces of the Traditionalist experience? It does not. First, a Traditionalist position constantly refers to ignorance, which is its analog, and as individuals remain stuck in its prefabricated norms [a vegetative state, apologism of stupidity, of the futile, etc.], the desire for truth and criticism are exiled to the sphere of what is unhealthy, through conformity, in short, through error. Tradition is persistent and has proven to be so throughout history.

Retabulist criticism can thus be formed with the idea of a mental revolution, a change of habit, a systematic and comprehensive rejection of internalized Traditionalism. It is necessary that the mind become [somewhat] arbitrary, intellectually - placed to a certain degree at the crossroads of the intelligible and the pragmatic. It is due to its arbitrary ancestry that Tradition [in the same way as sectarian currents, religious or philosophical] is found to be not only an irrational arbiter, but also a constraint in the experience of mankind's history. The thought which must be arrived at in any meditation on Tradition, is the endeavor to give a dialectical response to critical modes of thought, in which reason [theoretical and theological] is inscribed - in short, this is a dialectic that reconciles a theology of Retabulism with an arbitrary Tradition.

The dialectical conception of theological Retabulism is not only an example, among others, of a dialectical solution to a Traditionalist problem that leads to criticism; it is in many ways the core reasoning, the lynch-pin, of the entire Retabulist system.

Theological Retabulism has the power to distance itself with respect to the Tradition and arise in pure, Universal reflection. At the same time, theological Retabulism remains a peculiarity in that it reflects itself and, thereby, reflects ontological universality.

In the concept of the universal and the discrete [the self-] arises the ability to identify oneself as an individual, as part of causation.

This dialectical schematic is enough to warn that theological Retabulism will be conceivable only if the subject of conceptualization can be considered dialectically; what we refer to as historicity is articulated in speech, out of which science extracts logic, not as a formal and empty structure, but the logic of being, that is to say, ultimately, ontological discourse. At all levels of discourse of theological historicity, Retabulism effectively certifies its dialectical character.

8 - *Supratheology: Schism and Heresy*

Retabulism makes very clear the distinction between theology and Tradition, although the latter mistakes itself for the former and even excludes to the end of acting as as the sole metaphysical reference. Theological Retabulism breaks with the habits of tradition, claiming at the same time the legitimacy of supratheology. It is clear, for example, that Tradition is sure to assign qualifiers to the Retabulist, i.e. schismatic and heretic. If an individual perceives faith in a supratheological manner, he is naturally considered to be heretical by the Guardians of Tradition [Traditionalists]. Traditionalism protests the supratheological appurtenance of Retabulism, and causes it to exist on the margins; since it was formally rejected by the Tradition, it inevitably creates a schism, or, at the very least, a rival faith.

Each [person] is comforted by his respective position as supporter or opponent of the Tradition.

a - *The Traditionalist Conviction*

It is clear that the [verbal and physical] repressive measures of Traditionalist authorities assault the defenders of *supratheology*, considered heretics. In addition to excluding them, they index their writings, their projects, and their actions.

Retabulism warns against Tradition and ideological currents by unveiling this representation of the error of doctrines deemed perverse and futile. The intervention of Retabulism is crucial to expose and destroy this exploitation of man and emphasize the stultifying, even devilish, origin of their opinions and their mores.

Retabulism demonstrates that Traditionalist dogma is one radically foreign to a *supratheological* reality which puts society and a genuine relationship with the divine as its central theme. In the name of a great future, Tradition drafted a project of mass smothering, purveying fear, torment, submission, punishment, curses, etc. This is to say nothing of the sects that were derived from it and that compete with it in their lies and absurdity. Indeed, these are an instrument with which Tradition dispenses [projects] an immense reductive power: it can introduce into a single set of information, under the name of God, its particular interests and non-theological motives.

There was never a suggestion for a debate that led to the rise of supratheological reflection. The content of Traditionalist faith was deployed, first "*intellectually*" and timidly in the middle of the 11th century, then massively at the start of the 14th century due to the decline of formal *Classical Islamic Civilization*. All which opposed the Traditionalist dogma were considered heretical theses and thus condemned. This policy is perpetuated in confessional historiography, which remains a monolithic socio-cultural institution whence the Tradition unfailingly immobilizes.

This fact remains true in the centuries that followed, attested to by the state of ruin of societies *prevailing on Islam* continually discoursing upon the Messenger of God, deifying the former and humanizing the latter. The Traditionalist policy is to think of the divine only in an ancillary way.

God this mysterious unknown [*Sic*]*!*

IV - Retabulism of a Universal Order: Being in the service of Humanity

A - *The Idealo-Realism of Retabulism*

The Retabulist is both an enterprising *idealist*[16] and a *realist*[17] or *ideo-realist* [*idealo-realist*]. It privileges human reason because of its responsibility as the steward of History.

Retabulist doctrines are distinguished by their unique didactic tact and their ingenious dialectic. Retabulism's value is mainly critical and it thus constructively enriches Knowledge by becoming a civilizational vector. It is the great destroyer of error, of falsehood, lies, inauthenticity, non-reality, of the irrational, etc.

Today, the deconstruction of consciousness, as well as epistemological anarchism, discourses of ignorance, financial apologism, sociological phenomena of rejection/compromise, the explosion of religious intolerance, etc. are manifestations leading down a path towards the decomposition of human reason. This [reason] is formatted by subjective tendencies, even though

---

[16] *Idealist*. Supporter of Realism, which is any philosophy that gives life to the idea, thoughts, considered in particular or in general.
[17] *Realist*. Supporter of Realism, which affirms the existence of an objective reality that objects to an exclusively phenomenological or formally scientific conception.

civilizational progress affirms objective tendencies [communication, development, etc.].

Belief in the reality of what is revealed by Knowledge is a normal, natural reaction on the part of the Retabulist. Indeed, this latter considers an intuitive element such as common sense, reason, etc., to be a principle of the real world. The distinction between the phenomenon [a fact, event, accessible by means of the senses] and the noumenon [objects of rational knowledge or science] represents a first step towards Retabulism. But it is constituted only when the world or universe is defined as the representation of a conscience or an intelligent and active subject.

Retabulism has been prepared, through its reflection on the nature of the relationship between intelligence and reality, which it conducts out of its opposition to the unintelligent and the false. The Retabulist idea takes shape through a representation, of an individual, a society, civilization, etc. Having a formal reality, or formal existence, is equivalent to being in a - universal - medium. Retabulism does not bracket the world or give it borders, as it is representative of cognition and, without it, there would be no reality outside the represented concept.

A reference to Deity [God, Creator of the Universe] is a guard against folly and a source of ideas that serves as a surrogate for an ontological reality: the insignificance of man, and by extension, all of humanity, in relation to the Universal. Retabulism ; authentic communion in the interest of reaching consensus by rising above the emotions to reside in the field of intelligible knowledge.

What is the significance of this notion? God does not think for man and does not think like him !

Before the appearance of Science in the 9th century, man had no knowledge about the universe beyond false impressions drawn from naive interpretations made on a sensory basis rather than on real ideas and distinct relationships of *cause-and-effect*; mankind lacked a science describing the laws of natural phenomena, free of irrationality - of magic - hence requiring true, Retabulist knowledge.

The problem of the mystification of concepts and ideas occupies an important place in Retabulism. All forms of dogmatism keep their eye on the concept of Retabulism because the former's requirement for accepted absolute objectivity is that it be chimerical, and it opposes a reasonable subjectivity, made functional.

Retabulism is a perpetual struggle against the erroneous idea, against a justification of interests, against passions shaded by an attitude removed from reality. Ultimately, any doubtful speech or proposal falls within the Retabulist protocol. For the Retabulist, opposing thought [institutional, dogmatic, etc.] may either remain static or metastasize in an atmosphere of false consciousness. Therefore, there is no question, in this context, of whether the category of criticism ought to be applied to the more explicit [opposing forms of thought].

Dogmatism [historical, historiographical, theological, etc.] turned toward the past and saw itself investing in social conservatism as a static function, while Retabulism turned toward the future, as a dynamic revolutionary or innovative factor.

1 - *Retabulism and Functional Construction of Consciousness*

At a time when the sterile and arbitrary rule, it is necessary to exclude from the outset any form of dogmatism which is tied to the soil of ignorance, nationalism, fanaticism, to a fascist ideology. Retabulism is a process the thinker accomplishes consciously, albeit prompted by real mobilizing forces that set in motion his intellectual abilities. With its logic and its clarificatory rigor - in the representations it studies [facts, events, phenomena, ideas, appropriate concepts] - Retabulism is a system with an important role in the life of the individual and, in a given society, a historical role. Without broaching the problem of a society's relationship to its own [cultural, ideological, socio-economic, etc.] past, Retabulism, as an explanatory system, incorporates science [in that the socio-functional [social reality] variable is made to agree with the theoretical [knowledge].

By Retabulism, what is meant is interpretations of the status quo that are a product of concrete experiences, a kind of rational knowledge, and so, authentic experiences. These are used in turn to discern the state of actuality and thus affect the individual and his society as emancipatory. In this regard, the divine plays a central role in Retabulist thought by capturing, via real knowledge, the Deity and is better able to transcend its own ego, avoiding getting lost in the maze of futility, the error of mystification. It is in this sense that it is a question of Emancipation, ontologically.

What can be more liberating than the liberation of the human to approach the divine !

Whatever one may say, the *science of the divine* is nothing else but *Science* [of natural laws] and it is through the latter that man grasps the nuances that illuminate the divine. With a science of the divine, it is a global system of interpretation of the [Historico-Event] Universe that serves to give direction to individual and collective action, toward the responsible. Indeed, Man, the Universe, derives not from chance, atomic accidents, or random biochemical reactions; it was not created in vain. It has authentic history; and the history of Man [which Retabulism demonstrates] can be neither distorted nor corrupted, because its actions and reactions fall under the immutable and irreversible designation of Event. They are evidence that, due to God, transcends human reason. Retabulism is a complex set of ideas and [scientific] representations that interprets the historical world, the world of historiography, theology, metaphysics, in an anti-dogmatic manner, and thus distances itself from illusion. Checking whether a thought is Retabulist is equivalent to disclosing error, unmasking *Disorder*; designating it so, thus reproaching it as false and fraudulent.

The term "*disorder*" means confusion, unrest; the chaos that affects the natural order of things, that is, of society and Man, of the ecosystem. In this sense, disorder is the absence of the divine [which gives meaning to life, to existence], the lack of regularity in the social, economic, political order, how the world is arranged.

Finally, "*disorder*" is that which makes it so that the individual loses his bearings, cannot find himself, and consequently submits to hormonal stimuli. It is up to him to escape the shadow of ignorance, of finance, Immorality, since he is taught that he is an animal appearing, by chance, on earth, and that he has only to answer to human laws.

The Retabulist point of view indicates that the established *disorder* aims to in fact draw out the state of things which has been pre-established. Retabulism denounces this Manichaean quality that instills a devaluation of all struggles against its interest - this diabolization of the adversary.

Modern thought formulates a collaboration between Retabulism and a vision of the world can be fruitful only if it explains that historico-historiographical Dogmatism is an externalization of an unhistorical scheme. This plot is but one aspect of a much larger phenomenon concerning, among others, the field of *psychopathology*, or *sociopsychiatry*[18].

a - Retabulism and Historicism

Retrospection is Retabulist, and thus true knowledge. In fact, it very well begins with Retabulism insofar as primacy of the present -methodologically- is allowed: a Retabulist historian chooses, as a function of actual criteria

---

[18] *Socio-psychiatry.* Study of mental unrest as a function of subjects belonging to a social group.

[tantamount to selecting scientifically], inquiries to pose the past [and present]. This process implies that historical reality suffered misinformation to the degree that conditional variables far and away from the view of consciousness were introduced.

Once society split by caste, order, or status, Retabulism - as reference - revealed the full extent of its utility. From the critical point of view, there is a parallel between traditional slavery, totally free of utopian notions, and that of 21 century finance, of egalitarian illusion. There is no warrant for considering the past as a kind of *propaedeutic*[19] for a privileged present, without introducing the hypothesis of a "*forged*" or "*fabricated*" meaning to History.

- *Resistance to change*

A scientific Retabulist concept can play the part of an ideological appeal. In this case, Retabulism is a factor in the resistance to the ever increasing power of the *culturo-financial* or *ideo-financial* system. This concept aims to uncover whether society is composed of a balanced or hierarchical system. Social dynamics would be more "*human*" in this sense; if they helped explain mutations in the social organization. For doctrinal significance, the importance of resisting mental paralysis and behavioral inertia [acquired habits] - i.e. false conscientiousness, intellectual laziness, moral complacency - should be kept in mind.

---

[19] *Propaedeutic*. Knowledge of elements constituting the necessary preparation for further study of one of the sciences.

The Retabulist project [intellectual, social, cultural, political, etc.] is not the conveyor of any kind of secret about a perfect society. It is a fact that structural changes are not well understood, and are easily attributed to the *Other*, which, in practice, presents as xenophobia or even *ostracism*[20]. This mentality still exercises influence on the political thought of most human societies overtook by fear and enveloped in ignorance.

For didactic reasons, recourse to the term "*historical distortion*" to underscore the perception of historical causality [historical events] seems sensible!

By simplifying somewhat the facts of the problem, its historical causality can be determined due to its Retabulist character, in the sense that events and historical facts are selected based on the circumstances and according to irrational prejudices.

b - Retabulism and Truth

There remains the important question of how Truth relates to Retabulism. Retabulism has, as an additional vocation, the elegant resolution of any historical or historiographical difficulty. Hence, admitting the universal origin of Western societies in the *Civilization of Classical*

---

[20] *Ostracism.* Decision to put or keep out of a society, a community, by discriminatory measures. Hostile attitude of a number of people constituting a community toward those of whom they disprove of. The action of excluding a political group, of keeping away from power, a person or group of persons; results of this action.

Islam in no way diminishes the scientific value of the concept of *Islam*. Actually, the story of Knowledge has a lot of implications for epistemology. Only the instrumentalization of historical theory is problematic so far as its factor of credibility. The supratheological approach can play a positive role in setting the stage for a scientific approach, and vice versa. Supratheological curiosity elicits a motivation that often persists after passion subsides, and can encourage studies of great scientific value.

What are the boundaries that separate the pursuit of [scientific] truth from the complacency of error? Returning the individual to Retabulist work, in the interest of answering the above query, note that scientific investigation is meant to simplify what is complicated, to render it accessible to the individual. Far from the usual intellectual comfort that is offered, accession of the masses in this respect proves hypothetical; and the reason for this is common sense - as tricky to codify in the concrete as in the abstract.

From a Retabulist perspective, the event or historical fact is what actually transpired at a certain time and a specific place. Its reality is established from a particular chain of causes or precursory conditions attained via various means of investigation [archaeological, anthropological, physical, etc.]. Retabulism shows that the history of non-European societies should no longer be deemed trivial - and consequently doomed to finish in oblivion.

One can distinguish in our societies two types of knowledge of events: one oriented towards the past, toward pre-established history. The other, toward Retabulism - toward History, restored!

If historical Retabulism seeks to string together past events in logical discourse, thus would true knowledge be constituted for the contemporary individual's practical existence. The prospective of the Retabulist evokes this sort of past proposal set in place, or those exposed and analyzed by anthropology, sociology and archeology.

Note that Retabulism is a new way of thinking, it is the response of Humanity, rendered anxious by the diversity of means of communication and the multitude of data that these communicate. As a consequence, the mechanism of relief for the anxiety of "*informations*" uncertainty, along with History, entrenches falsehood and manipulation instead of evolving towards truth. Its core function is to enlighten us. History has shown us enough of its inconsistencies, the engineers of confusion.

The individual forewarned by Retabulism may change, to some extent, the perception of himself and his society through his rational response, which figures it is preferable to not remain passive against the backdrop of events imagined possible or probable. On one hand, this means that the discourse of Retabulism tends to deny events hidden behind regularities; on the other, it reveals the quest for truth promoted by Retabulism, i.e. to make from modern history an act of creation in terms of human freedom!

Finally, Retabulism proceeds from a typology of events and the correspondence among these as well as that which each has with other forms of evidence [archaeology, ethnology, etc.]. Initially limited to the domain of history, historiographical and religious Retabulist efforts naturally must become much more ambitious. They tend to affect all areas and have long term goals. Based on its nature and scope, Retabulism is a process, a reflexive model that situates its efforts opposing those of Orthodox [or formal] History and its speculations.

The Retabulist position is explained by advances in processes of knowledge and the increasingly urgent need for individuals to make decisions that are informed by the future—often in the long term since the future of their offspring is at stake. This interest is generated not only from social and cultural reasons which are not novel, but also economic and political ones. Therefore, mere curiosity is no longer enough, because what is needed is far more than a flight from the present; it is a radical change in the perception and implementation of events, in the course of the life of the individual.

The Retabulist individual must emancipate himself in a real way from anxieties and hopes which draw their essence from the emotional and imaginary nature of fears and tired dreams, in order to generate a very real awareness of the present reality. To do so, it is essential that she reassess and alter the discourse, the [highly controversial] proposals of the propagandists and supporters of *Disorder*[21].

---

[21] *Disorder:* In areas such as overcrowding, the catastrophic deterioration of the environment, alienation of the individual through over-consumption and its application in the form of mental bondage, the intoxication perpetrated by media, genetic degradation, the manipulation of biology, psychology in humans, the seizing of decision-making power [political,

c - Retabulism of He who Reflects

The political and financial determinists want total control of the future. It is an area that we are not suspicious of, even if we deign to develop interest through a careful investigation, one which Retabulism pursues. Such an investigation regards *History* [in general], an octopus lurking in the shadows of Culture and Education, which extends its tentacles to snap up credulity, confidence, emotion, the very reason for all that, makes the individual. His hunting grounds: the Humanities and Theology.

Sometimes one believes what one reads [of Orthodox or "official" History] because those in the service of the State [Historians] are believed to be the erudite scholars responsible for writing it [Historiography], but this is not true.

Conversely, it often happens that historical writings appear improbable because they do not meet the criteria prescribed by [official] history, while these, in fact, are true. The inevitable is sometimes only a disguised desire to sow disorder, to better rule, which impresses on the insufficiently informed opinion or those individuals

---

social, economic, cultural] by only a few financial executives, and the highly technocratic nature of this power, etc. True, technology has liberated from onerous tasks, engineered triumphs over diseases, raised standards of living, contributed to changes in leisure, improved arrangements of nature, increased universalization, communication between men and, more generally, the qualitative elevation of existence and of human possibilities. The key is not to deny Disorder, but to compare it to the steps of Humanity, to address its accessibility, use, management, etc.

stressed by the risks of everyday existence. *Is this not the purpose intended, and disavowed by certain strategists?*

It is undeniable that if we did not manipulate History by rewriting it or fabricating it, the face of the world would be different!

The Retabulist thought appears to have a field that never ceases to expand. Thanks to resources currently available to it, including the tools of communication and computer science and thanks to advances in methods of investigation and more generally, to the scientific disciplines of which it avails, it [the Retabulist thought] can alter, highlight, predict and plan rational conduct for all historical and historiographical action.

Consequently, the Retabulist work, to a large degree, can prepare the individual by making him conscientious of this being the right direction to enable him to prepare a better future than s\he has been offered. Indeed, henceforth, he finally has free will because Truth is distinguished from error immediately!

Retabulism raises a fundamental question of choice between ends. One thing is certain, the 1% will not be responsible for fixing things. The "*Guardians of Retabulism*" watch over constitutions [doctrines and ideologies] that aim to control the future. How can we ensure that it [the future] is made viable and livable for all? On the other hand, to admit that this agreement is fulfilled by ends alone leaves to be prepared the program that is willing to achieve them. In any case, there is so much uncertainty, so many lies, so many patent falsehoods that one wonders if a good and program can even be established. By admitting it may be one such program, Retabulism will have to maintain, in the realization of its ends, all its principles [truth, authenticity in action, upholding the common good, etc.].

Thus, from the outset, Retabulism proves to be a particularly difficult enterprise, in that it must unite very different approaches [cultural, socio-economic, spiritual, intellectual, etc.].

2 - *Retabulism and the Future of Human Society*

The processes which use Retabulism to restore Truth suggest that it know clearly where it has to go and how to get there and that it is capable of reaching conclusions of certainty. Moreover, as designated, Retabulism could serve as a new force. Indeed, in many respects, especially its own character lies the fact that it considers, with a view to the future, the various aspects of human society.

Retabulism offers patently scientific traits - the general characteristics of scientific knowledge - intending to take care of past events that have been mutilated, forged, fabricated in systematic, methodical fashion, and as rigorously as possible. All this in order to guide instill in the societies of today respect for abiding truth and authenticity -and wisdom, for its part- to open doors of dialogue and reconciliation regarding an intelligent future that is surely very different, but at the same time, carrying much commonality.

Retabulism assumes that the individual who reasons knows how to free himself from mindsets, prejudices, cultural categories that shape his vision, but that the future can no longer accept as *Humanity* aspires to the same ideal of emancipation. It is above all this development that forms Retabulism and that deserves much wider and bolder acceptance, as it installs possibilities of a methodical investigation of reality/truth in the service of the future, in "*Service of Humanity*".

While playing a large part in general dispositions, such as emotions, intuitions, pragmatism, Retabulism nevertheless adopts precise ways of operating that maintain its scientific, that is, rational, character. It proceeds to compiling an inventory of facts, as completely as possible. It rigorously examines actual situations. Retabulism strives to use the intentions, the motivations of behavior, individual and collective. It seeks to attain the most essential phenomena, inherent to reality, logic, reason, which remain the key variables in Retabulist consciousness. It develops blueprints, authentic historical, historiographical, theological models of the future.

The Retabulist process arises from a model that corresponds with the nature of life in a society. Its investigation is first, a factual science, positive; second, a science of action, normative.

Exploring in all measures possible ways of recognizing the future, given the facts of the present, Retabulism is led to committing its attention to categories of fact from the past, to isolate those that determine the future. The heavily deceitful tendencies [made so as consequence of being constituted by a range of pseudo-historical or dogmatic facts [of Orthodox or "*official*" history]] that determine what contemporary society becomes today, coupled with Retabulist reflection, serve to predict, with negligible risk of error: the evolution of thought, the rhythm of technical progress, of communication, an obstinance of curiosity, of certain habits of the inquiries of the individual, etc. Retabulist facts portentous of the future, often perceptible, constitute realities, initially embryonic, certainly, but the importance of which will not tarry in being affirmed, that will naturally have a profound and extensive impact.

The vocation and purpose of Retabulism is therefore to pose the larger and most fundamental question of its relationship with History. Does the Retabulist consider the future an extension or rather restoration of the past? Actually, the future according to Retabulists is [with good reason] to break with the traditional tendency to think of the future as a continuation of a corrupt past. But to create the future, must we completely let go of this past? So powerful are the pressures currently exerted by the new, that even tamed by Retabulism, a tension will still be felt between a past, albeit one that does not speak its name and wishes to continue so, and the institutions, customs, the Tradition; all these hope to endure, and innovative Retabulist forces prescribe how to overcome them. An antagonism exists between *the past which must be restored* and *a future which must be established*. The latter must lead to the correction, or at worst to the eradication of the former. This is to preserve from the past only the authentic, truthful, knowing well that many aspects are obsolete, while others are manufactured and maintained with singular force. Ignorance of this fact, which Retabulism has always denounced, has always seriously distorted our vision of the future.

The future as seen by Retabulism is observed in categories of problems, structures, interactions, processes, of which identification and characterization are often, formally at least, of a different nature than that which the past produced. The Retabulist experience and method, especially in the comprehensive form of history, can also be useful to formulate the future. As far as a future that needs to be established, however, Retabulism comprises a highly creative enterprise. It has control of its actions in a manner as rational and consistent as possible, but at the same time, it needs to make use of all resources in the spirit of creativity.

Thus in the method dubbed *Retabulist*, imagination and reason intersect where all assumptions involved in the implementation of the sustainability of economic, cultural, and social factors are conceived, the Retabulist process is made viable by unearthing, restoring, admitting. Therefore, is the proposed future much more likely simply by virtue of being a future whose realization is assured on new bases of truth and sincerity, its precious guides; thereafter, it will be possible to locate other developments, other policies, other objectives.

However, the easiness along which Retabulism is conducted should be paired with caution, because Retabulism prefers certainty to conjecture, it ought to remain vigilant with respect to the accumulation of proposals or facts to be measured against reality.

As far as the extent of the area covered by Rétablisme, "*Service of Humanity*" is presented in a global form that embraces the totality of the future, that is to say, all humanity, all components of life and the activities of man.

This is the project of the [Retabulist] reflection that takes on all areas in a clean approach, aiming to capture the overall dynamism carrying humanity into the future. For this, Retabulism assumes the apprehension of several factors and interactions which reveal the diversity of situations actually covered: concepts of consumer society, industrial civilization, liberal society, government institutions and administration, business, education, conception of authority, of family, of lifestyle, etc.

a - The Outlook of Retabulism

Retabulism prioritizes certain factors, such as the evolution of civilization and more broadly, the increasing challenges levied against society that reveal the number of structures and behaviors thought to form the immutable framework of society [Tradition, customs, etc.], which are likely to experience profound transformations, due to misinformation of the media, poisoning of the mind by all media and institutionalized cerebral formatting in areas as diverse as social, cultural and ideological forms, along with the tensions and conflicts resulting from these. Challenging a certain idea of irrational passion that sociological phenomena turns down and rejects also suits Retabulism; it takes into account social and cultural aspirations, values and ideologies in all their diversity so long as they are genuine.

Do we attend to a decline of ideologies advocating technical and economic predominance, or do these ideologies encompass a technological and economic influence on society ?

Retabulism thinks his approach will almost certainly lead to a development of awareness, once the individual questions the global, reflexive, and systematic nature of the future of society, and by extension, of civilization. Such a question is always part of the debate opened by Retabulism, between scientific knowledge and philosophical and religious knowledge. By extending such an invitation, Retabulism acts as host to a reconciliation that may have the appearance of integration or union.

The ambition, so to speak, of Retabulism is that it devotes itself to the creation of large, genuine interdisciplinary centers, able to implement an ambitious scientific policy and give to history its credentials on scientific and institutional foundations.

It would not be illusory were international journals, scientific societies, conferences, and annual gatherings beginning to form a partly interdisciplinary, international network of communication to escape the human experience that is a History constituted by the fortress of *Dogmatism*.

Currently, there is considerable confusion in the way the terms "*History and Historiography*" are used. Retabulism, in its broadest sense, gathers under this language [History, Historiography] all scientific approaches to cognition, whether historical or historiographical their accomplishment.

On the side of Retabulist thought, of an intellectual or religious order, we are inclined to discern in Retabulism an investigation with concrete, particular traits that concern the future of society, and that, therefore, interfere with speculative theories or doctrines of "Disorder" [financial and political] which intend to - at the fundamental level of the existence of the individual - express not only meaning but direction !

Retabulism takes to increasing the significance of changes, brought about most notably through scientific or technical progress, which in the present state of things [tending toward "Disorder"] renew only timidly the human condition, the rootedness of the state of man and his ecosystem. Retabulists tend to see the considerations of civilizational progress as views worthy of attention. The critical attitude of Retabulism should be accentuated in proportion to the intensification of the workings and ever-growing power of the "harms" that pose a threat to Humanity. However, the opposition between Retabulist thinkers and their opponents, which met because the future of human societies needs to be determined [future, choices, etc.], especially when it examined from a global point-of-view; of interpretative problems, responsibility, meaning and orientation.

Particularly, when decisions that guide the future of society impose on behalf of Finance, Policy, widespread misinformation or simply because of the State. In a liberal world, this determination of Retabulism inevitably lead to confrontation. Few Ideologies, whatever these may be [spiritual extremism, materialism, liberalism, etc.], agree to be questioned by Retabulism, but they intend to keep their hegemony, so as to be the authoritative guides. Such claims are definitely founded in ignorance and the indoctrination of those who adhere to it. Still, it is sufficient that Retabulist reason lead by presenting information [historical, historiographical, theological, etc.] that is not presented forcibly, as it would be from another ideology, were it scientific [rational, authentic].

3 - Themes or topics that may be addressed by Retabulism

Establishing *historical Order* by restoring *historiographical Disorder* is one ability of *Retabulism*. Countless are the false, corrupt, or just plain made up facts and historical events, gathered over the centuries [the Middle Ages, the Renaissance, the Enlightenment, the Industrial Age, and the Colonial Period]. These are commonly accepted by the collective consciousness, as imposed by education, academia, society, popular culture, and most recently, in a colossal and chaotic way, through social networks [Internet].

The need to open up Retabulism to a greater number [of individuals] should be emphasized. All people are responsible for the future of their society; each citizen must engage in the search for Truth, and be heard in the consideration of decisions orienting History [of Man and her society], which belongs, sans pretention, to the whole of humanity.

It is undeniable that Retabulism might give itself, as straightforward objective, the identification, observation and analysis of the most detailed and general aspects of *History* and *Historiography*, at their source. We note here, in a list of already considerable length, some themes/topics with self-explanatory titles.

a - Some Prospective Retabulist Tracks

- *Prehistory*

- The Origins of Man : approaches other than evolution or mechanistic theories, etc.
- Migration of Mankind on Earth: origins and the formation of displacement.
- Tools, crafts, architecture, navigation, etc. Origins and development.
- Writing System: origins and development.
- Etc., etc.

- *Antiquity*

- The Greco-Roman societies: reality; historically.
- Figures of Antiquity : reality; historically.
- Origins of Science: reality; historically.
- Life and customs of ancient societies: reality; historically.
- Judaism, Christianity [and the Church]: reality; historically.
- Charlemagne, Charles Martel: reality; historically. The monumental buildings: Origins -reality; historically.
- Etc., etc.

- *Middle Ages and Renaissance*

- Life of the Moors and Feudal Society : reality; historically.

- Islam and pseudo-Islam [Tradition : Hadiths] : reality; historically.
- Crusades : objective. Reality; historically.
- Renaisance : reality; historically.
- Native Americans: reality; historically.
- The Ottomans: Who were they and what did they actually accomplish.
- Reality; historically - regarding their "*Khalifat*".
- Etc., etc.

- *Enlightenment*

- Western Rationalism, Science and technology : reality; historically.
- Treatment of non-Caucasians, industrialization: reality; historically.
- Great Treasures in Europe: origins and development. Reality ; historically.
- Etc., etc.

- *Modern Era*

- Civil War of the United States of America : reality; historically.
- The French Revolution: origins and repercussions. Reality ; historically.
- Agents of the French Revolution: Who are they : reality; historically.
- The movement of the culture of Classical Islamic Civilization to the West : imitation, plagiarism: reality; historically.
- Great Explorers of the West: Were they really so? : reality; historically.

- Who Really Discovered America ? : Discovery of America and contact with Indigenous Peoples.
- Napoléon Bonaparte: Who was he really : reality; historically.
- Napoléon Bonaparte and World Finance: reality; historically.
- Napoléon Bonaparte and the Egyptian Campaign: the code of Napoléon : reality ; historically.
- Colonisation of the World and Global Industrialisation : reality; historically.
- Colonisation of Algeria: reality ; historically.
- Decolonization and Finance: reality; historically.
- International, [Europe, Globalization] Political and Financial Organizations : reality; historically.
- Wars [14-18, 39-45] : reality ; historically.
- The Crisis of 1929 - International Finance : reality ; historically.
- Globalization, and its True Objectives : reality; historically.
- Etc., etc.

Annex

Hadith

Means an oral communication, words supposed to have been uttered, and the actions alleged to have been carried out by Mohammed, the transmitter of the message of Islam. In the 10th and 11th century, these alleged statements were compiled in book form [Bukhari& Muslim, Al-Nawawi, etc.] and served as an opportunity for each consecutive generation of saint, spiritual "guide", religious leader, Imam, or Traditionalist [or Hadithist] to complete it with additions. Like the Talmud these collections include all of what is called Tradition that purports to be related to the actions and words of Mohammed and his companions. This Tradition was originally imposed in the 14th century by socio-political [caliphs, viziers, sultans, etc.] and spiritual [Imams, Ulemas, Muftis, etc.] authorities, enforced under penalty of, on the one hand, a divine curse; and on the other, sanctions for disobedience, as principles of both a personal and collective governance for Muslims. The hadiths were reported by tens of thousands of companions [Ismail Ibn Kathir, "As-Sira". Edit. Universal, 2007, p. 927]. [in the text]

The hadiths form what is improperly called the Sunna. Some authors have identified more than 700,000 hadiths. All these quotes, sayings, and stories institutionalized the Hadith, before its being imposed and disseminated throughout the Muslim empire, and thus were the principal cause of the ruin [intellectual, cultural, social, spiritual, etc.] of the Muslims.

According to the Rabbis, Moses received two revelations of the Lord. The first, in text, the Torah, is too complex, too esoteric for the Jew or the common man. So, an explanation or exegesis was divinely revealed in the form of a compilation: the Talmud. The course of religious instruction is institutionalized; it has been studied and transmitted from Rabbi to Rabbi in a continuous chain. The Talmud is the Oral Law [or oral Torah]. Its books contain the substance, particularly the code which consists of the Mishnah ["Hadith" in Palestinian or Babylonian] along with its exegesis, or [Palestinian or Babylonian] commentary, Gemara ["Sunna" or acts]. According to Traditionalists, Muhammad received two revelations from God. One, in written form, the Koran [Qur'an] is too complex, too esoteric for the Muslim or the common man. God then revealed his explanation or exegesis in the form of a compilation; the collection of Hadiths or Tradition [Michna]. Religious instruction is institutionalized, studied and transmitted from Traditionalist to Traditionalist along an unbroken chain.

Tradition is the Oral Law [or oral Koran]. According to the Traditionalists, it represents all of the books that contain that which is of substance, particularly the constituted code, again according to Traditionalists; the Koran [Qur'an] and its exegesis or commentary [Meccans and Medinans] comprise Tafseer. The fundamental principle of Qur'anic content, ignored or neglected by Traditionalists, is "Being in service of Humanity." This is what great men, the Muslims from the 8th to 13th century, understood and disseminated. These men were in the service of the World. Torches illuminating the real world, they created the Civilization of Classical Islam [CIC] not exclusively to the welfare of Muslims, but all humanity. This period, from the 8th to the 13th century, was under the rule of the Qur'an, which inspired men to be better and helped them to exit the darkness of mankind's ignorance into the light of Science, creating progress in the scientific, technical, socio-economic, and cultural, so that men and women could devote themselves to the message of Islam: "Being in service of humanity" which is the ultimate form of worship that God not only approves of, but recommends above all. The rest is simple ritual - prayer, fasting, pilgrimage, zakat. How reliable are the five "pillars" of ritual? Merely accessory, if not in the service of Humanity [via goodness, generosity, altruism, respect, etc.] of which we are the foundation, par excellence. The period of the advent of Islam, the 8th to 13th centuries. And the big names are still coming! Afterward, the 13th to 21st centuries, represents the advent of Tradition, the Talmud of Anti-Solomons. This was the reign of the Hadith or Tradition. Islam in the Qur'an is abandoned and discarded. Tradition is the religious source, mental course of action, the main principle governing thought. Thus, in the shade of caliphs, sultans and viziers, an Order of Traditionalists, like that of an initiated Masonic Order, governs Muslims and their societies. History attests to the state of ruin of societies called Muslim. The "Sheikhs," the "Mufti," the "Imams," the "Ulama," gesticulating wildly and emptily in various media are Traditionalists, i.e. professionals of Tradition [Hadith] which is the Talmudic prototype. As do Jews who base their religion not on the Torah but on the Talmud, the practical basis of all Traditionalists is the Tradition [Hadith]. This is the problem that arises at the dawn of the 21st century. These Sheikhs, Muftis, Ulemas and Imams carry the same slogan: "Muslims do not understand Islam and do not practice correctly." In fact, neither they nor many of those who call themselves "Muslims"-understand Islam and Qur'anic content because the Anti-Solomonic collection, the Tradition of the Talmud, pre-formats the mind of anyone who approaches it. God addresses Traditionalists or the Guardians of Tradition: "Those who were charged with the Torah [Torah] but have not applied its teachings are comparable to a donkey carrying books. Evil is the similitude of people who falsify the Signs of Allah. And Allah guides not the Zalimoun [the unjust or insolent]. [Qur'an, 62-5] The "Chaykhs [Sheikhs]," the "Mufti," the "Imams," the "Ulema" are Arabic, and some learn the Qur'an by heart, but that is irrelevant as they are unable to grasp or apply its content; to put themselves in "service of Humanity." This verse speaks to and describes perfectly both the Anti-Solomonic providers of Tradition ["Hadith"] such as the Chaykhs, Muftis, Ulemas, Imams, etc., whose doctrines and recommendations are collectively followed by all the Anti-Solomonic. This verse is addressed to Jews do you say? Perhaps, but it so well characterizes the Anti-Solomonic because it does not mitigate or qualify its description of those who followed in the footsteps of the Jews that strayed. Indeed, in order to understand the significance of this verse in full, it is useful to "refresh" it, for didactic reasons, as follows: "Those who were charged the Qur'an [Koran] but who have not applied it [as instead, they follow Tradition, i.e. Hadith] are like a donkey carrying books [the donkey cannot grasp the content of books, it can only support their weight]. Evil is the similitude of people who falsify the Signs of Allah. And Allah guides not the Zalimoun people [the unjust, insolent] [by degrading and immersing others in degeneration and decay].

Conclusion

The Retabulism has a role to play in the understanding of modern societies in order to disclose their articulation no doubt with the real history, authentic in the aim to serve as a reference (mine of information] implementation between the hands of the social (as a science and as principles relating to the lives of men in society). In fact, the history is currently under the influence of the dizzying economy [Finance], and therefore of the "*economic reason*" which is endeavoring to never take into account, in the framework of the rationality [cognition] the ontological concept of the individual, yet fundamental element characteristic of the society.

The Retabulism as an ideology is an excellent model repository. But its adoption process of a free choice. In addition, the Retabulism may contribute to denounce the a priori, the views too artificial to be truthful, the resolutions too imprecise and the manufacture of historical concordismes of some philosophical currents and theological which lead to the world at its loss. The vivacity of mind retabulist is a valuable aid for those wanting to purify themselves from the mire of *institutionalized dogmatism* [cultural, social, spiritual] and to better define its methods and objectives in light of rebuild its vision of the world and therefore, its existence and its future.

In a more positive and constructive way, the Retabulism offers to the "philosophical" and theological reflection an ample food for thought, the invitation not to caulk in the misconceptions and irrational, especially in terms of the values and moral standards and, more generally, the human condition. Perhaps does he regard the concept "be in the service of humanity" as essential, highly metaphysical could we say!

Alphabetical index

A

Aesthetic, 36
Algoritmi, 54
Al-Khwarizmi, 54
Alterations, 41
Ancient Greece, 55
Anthropologist, 62
Anti-dogmatic, 101
Antiquity, 118
Anti-scientific, 42
Apologism, 92, 97
Architect, 62
Authentic, 53
Authenticity, 55
Axiomatic historical, 56

B

Bourgeoisie, 33

C

Civilization of Classical
    Islam, 124
Civilizational, 41
clarificatory rigor, 100
Classical Islamic Civilization,
    32, 57, 95
Classical Islamic Civilization
    [CIC], 53
Communication, 68
Conceptualization, 93
Conviction, 94

Cultural, 110

D

Deity, 98
Dialectical movement, 49
Discovering, 48
Disorder, 101
Divine, 101
Dogmatic history, 37
Dogmatism, 35, 36, 47, 102
Dumbing down, 81

E

Ecclesiastical, 33
Education, 67
Egyptologists, 62
Electron, 87
Electron microscope, 71
Emphasizes, 47
Empiricism, 43
Enlightenment, 119
Epistemological, 68
Epistemo-Retabulist, 87
Error, 92
Established global disorder,
    35

Establishment, 37
Ethical, 36
Eethical code, 63
Events, 61

F

Fable, 54
Facts, 61
False, 86
Falsehistoriography, 51
Falsehood, 40
Fathers of Tradition, 77
Folklore, 54
Freedom, 77
Future, 112

G

Garde-fou, 92
Geber, 54
Global knowledge, 37
God, 34, 95
Greco-Roman Heritage, 32
Greek antiquity, 63
Greek science, 57
Greek universe, 42
Greeks, 42

H

Hadith, 123
Hence, 57
Heretical, 95
Hippocrates, 54
Historeupean, 32
Historeupéocentrism, 32
Historian, 51
Historical, 36
Historical dogmatism, 55
Historical law, 58
Hhistorical Order, 117
Historical Retabulism, 52, 106
Historical Retabulism,, 55
Historical-theological, 80
Historicité, 38
Historico-historiographical, 102
Historiography, 49, 51, 65, 117
History, 51, 108, 117
Human, 63
Human Civilization, 52
Human reason, 97
Humanities, 79
Humanity, 47, 49, 74, 114

I

Idea, 72
Idealizing, 46
Ideo-financial, 103
Ideo-realist, 97
Ignorance, 33, 39, 44
Imams, 125
Imitators, 43
Immobilism, 33
Individuals, 117
Instrumentalization, 77
Intangible, 47
Intellectualist, 64
Islam, 95
Islamic, 72

J

Jabir Ibn Hayyan, 54

K

Khaliphal, 77
Knowledge, 37, 44, 64, 65, 84
Knowledge of God, 71
Koran [Qur'an], 124

L

Language, 48
Legend, 54
Logical-deductive, 42
Logicist, 79

M

Magical, 42
Manner, 43
Meaning, 40
Meanwhile, 36
Media, 49
Mental revolution, 92
Metaphysical ideation, 85
Metastasize, 99
Middle Ages, 118
Misinformation, 44
Modeling, 45
Modern Era, 119
Monarchs, 33
Monoscripts, 73
Mufti, 125
Muslim Empire, 76
Muslim lands, 77
Muslim thinkers, 59
Muslims, 43, 57
Mystification, 40
Mythological, 42

N

Noumenon, 98

O

Object of theoretical, 81
Obscurantism, 33
Observation, 45
Official, 112
Ontological universality, 93
Oral Law, 124
Order, 49
Orthodox, 66
Orthodox History, 32, 43
Orthrodox history/government, 32
Ostracism, 104
Ottomans, 77

P

Philosophy, 83
Physical, 83
Pragmatism, 35
Pragmatist, 45
Praxeological, 78
Prehistory, 118

R

Rational knowledge, 100
Reason, 47
Reductionism, 42
Reflects, 108
Relativises, 56
Religious, 75
Renaissance, 118
Resistance, 103

Retabulism, 110,
Retabulism position. Voir
Retabulism speech, 31
Retabulism thought. Voir
Retabulist, 31, 33, 112
Retabulist antithesis, 42
Retabulist criterion, 34
Retabulist knowledge, 90
Retabulist Values, 34

S

Salvation, 84
Schism, 94
Scholars, 43, 55
Science, 36, 42, 45, 68, 80, 82, 101, 124
Scientific, 54, 60
Scientific Retabulist, 103
Service of humanity, 34, 111
Sociological, 36
Solipsism, 39
Speculation, 78
Spiritual, 110
Strategists, 109
Superlogic, 35
Superstitious, 42
Supra-logical, 35
Supratheological, 88
Supratheology, 76, 81, 94

T

Talmud, 125
Telescope, 79
Theogony, 54
Theological, 36
Theological Retabulism, 71, 74
Theology, 69, 89
Though, 61
Tradition, 68, 75, 77, 83, 114
Traditionalism, 94
Traditionalist, 76, 86, 90
True historiography, 51
Truth, 40, 104

U

Universal, 98
Universal Culture, 33
Universal values, 41
Universalism, 33, 48
Utopia, 54

W

Well-being, 66
Western society, 59
Widespread, 44

Z

Zionist, 33